Writing your Own Worship Materials

Writing Your Own Worship Materials

- Responsive Readings • Litanies
- Prayers • Worship Service Outlines

G. Temp Sparkman

Judson Press ® Valley Forge

Writing Your Own Worship Materials

Copyright © 1980
Judson Press, Valley Forge, PA 19482-0851

Fifth Printing, 1993

Library of Congress Cataloging in Publication Data

Sparkman, Temp.
  Writing your own worship materials.

  Bibliography: p.
  1. Liturgies.   I.   Title.
BV176.S65   264   79-26126
ISBN 0-8170-0857-8

To John Claypool and Arnold Epley
who first affirmed me as a
worship leader

Foreword

The renewal of worship is a significant feature of contemporary Christian life. New styles have been introduced, especially through innovations in music and architecture. New themes have been developed, such as the offer of a liberating gospel to the oppressed. New emphases have appeared, notably the participation of the laity in general and of women in particular.

Congregations in the free church tradition have been at a disadvantage both in contributing to and in benefiting from this liturgical revival. Jealous to protect the hard-won right of freedom in worship from the prescribed formalisms of established churches, many evangelical denominations have been reluctant to sponsor consultations that would attempt a codification—other than in hymnody—of the rich service materials appearing in recent years. As a result, many choice contributions by individual worship leaders have gone largely unnoticed except in their local congregations and are destined to be short-lived for lack of any recognized anthology (i.e., any free church "Book of Common Prayer") to conserve the liturgical riches of our generation for those that follow.

It is, therefore, an occasion for rejoicing that Temp Sparkman has begun to fill this void both by sharing with us the fruit of his sensitive spirit and by teaching us how to be creative in a tradition where the freedom to be spontaneous and original so often sadly degenerates into the freedom to be hackneyed and trite. If in what follows he writes as a worship leader, then I write here as one who was led. During our years together in the Crescent Hill Baptist Church, Louisville, Kentucky, he served as a member of the ministerial staff while I served as a grateful if intermittent worshiper when not called away by duties as a seminary professor and administrator. This relationship provided abundant opportunity to see and hear in actual practice what this book can only report in literary form and so to experience firsthand the authenticity of the approach which it commends.

With an unerring sense of relevance, Sparkman has concentrated on the specific area where free church worship is most vulnerable to mediocrity. He rightly observes that worship consists of two "grand movements"—that of the worshiper to God and of God to the worshiper—and, not being a pastor/preacher, he is content to treat only the former, aware that a great host of works is already available dealing with sermon and Supper. Broadly speaking, Baptists in particular have long viewed a service as having two halves, the first half with which this work deals being slighted in favor of the dominant place of preaching in the second half. In fact, many pastors contemptuously referred to this first half of the service as "the preliminaries" until ministers of music gained enough clout to ban that wretched term.

One result of this heritage is that in many churches today music dominates the first half and preaching the second half of the service, each with its forceful leader, leaving everything else as transitional elements used to fill gaps between these "major" parts of the service. I know churches in which all week long the musician works on the anthem and the preacher on the sermon, but the prayers and readings are haphazardly assigned as the platform party is about to enter the sanctuary. I know other churches in which it is openly admitted that these "incidental" assignments are passed around to give lesser staff members more public exposure. All too often, the nonmusical elements in the first half of the service have become the neglected stepchildren of free church worship.

But it is precisely these elements on which Sparkman focuses his attention: the call to worship, invocation, pastoral prayer, offertory, responsive reading, and seasonal emphases. And how much he makes out of what others make so little! Far from being "filler material," these elements set the tone and point the direction for the entire service. They provide opportunities for introducing a presiding metaphor or dominant theme for the service. They may suggest theological ideas around which sermonic insights may be gathered. They liberate emotions which may then be expressed through carefully chosen hymns. They function much as the overture to a symphony in which a motif is sounded over and over before some mighty resolution is attempted at the climax.

Thus would I urge your careful reading and thoughtful

pondering of this book. But even more I would encourage you to be guided by the author's efforts to attempt your own well-crafted contributions. Most of us live prosaic lives, and so we stand in awe of anyone who dares to shape a thing of beauty as an offering for the Father. Yet surely there are more hidden wellsprings of creativity within us that the Spirit yearns to liberate than we have begun to realize (see John 7:38). What better place to fire the imagination than in a litany or prayer? Even if you must lavish your deepest devotions on so small an assignment, it will be worth the effort. Every great building needs its foyer. Every great ecstasy needs its foreplay. Just so, every great encounter with God in worship needs those "passages" that uplift with their loveliness, that sober with their seriousness, that clarify with their simplicity, that embolden with their confidence. Preaching and Communion are precarious ventures at best, but without such preparation as this they are reckless gambles indeed.

One caution: to follow the pathway marked out by Sparkman, you will need to do far more than read this book and spend the prescribed time for each exercise. The fruits on which we feast here are the harvest of a whole life-style of gentle modesty (which the author calls "reserve"). In reality, therefore, what we have here is the call to a contemplative stance which makes room for reflective brooding in the frantic pace of institutional religious life. Only those who have learned to stare in wonderment at nature, or to listen with relish to the babblings of a child, or to commune with the silences at midnight will ever be able to see glory lurking in the commonplace or hear the rustle of angels' wings.

William E. Hull
Pastor, First Baptist Church
Shreveport, Louisiana

Contents

Introduction

The Worship Event and These Materials

In the past few years we have seen a lively interest in worship materials which are more contemporary, spontaneous, and meaningful. The interest exists within both the free church and the liturgical traditions. In one there is a dissatisfaction with bland worship forms and with personality-centered worship. And in the other, the disenchantment is with staid, archaic worship materials.

Lay persons in churches where Reformation doctrine has stripped worship of its color and drama find it difficult to focus on the holy because of the lack of enabling symbols and the absence of objective content of real significance. Further, they feel a bankruptcy in worship because worship is, in the absence of a transcendent reality, too dependent on the personality of the preacher.

In liturgical churches lay persons wonder what relevance there is in the repetitions of worship. They want worship forms which engage their emotions and worship content which satisfies the intelligence.

Fortunately, worship can include both traditional and new approaches and still be meaningful. I have participated in worship which assumed a reasonable degree of form and still was alive and relevant. Thus, worship can be fresh while at the same time subscribe to some meaningful form. It can come from deep within the past, reflect a resonance with the present, and serve both emotion and intellect.

Effective worship consists of two grand movements—the worshiper to God and God to the worshiper. If these two dimensions seem wrongly ordered, let me quickly dispel any notion that we take the initiative in the God-worshiper relation. To the contrary, at bottom we understand that in creation, revelation, and incarnation God moves first toward us. It was he who in the garden story came in the cool of the day seeking Adam and Eve. And, likewise, he acted in revelation through the life of his Chosen People, Israel. And in Paul's theology this initiative is seen in the Christ who came to us while we were sinners.

However, the worship event begins with our movement toward God. These overtures are expressed in the call to worship, the prayer, the reading, and the offering. They assume that God has already spoken to us, moved in our direction, and invited us to respond. And, of course, the conversation and the movement are never simply one way; for regardless of who makes the first move, once the second party joins in, there is a mutuality. Thus, even in these elements of worship, which are primarily our movement toward God, he, too, is approaching us.

God's movement toward us may be said to be primarily through the Supper and the sermon. In one, he comes to us in mercy and hope, forgiving our sins and renewing our experience of faith, and in the other he comes in word to offer us perspective and guidance.

The Lord's Supper—Communion, Eucharist, or however it is termed—is not a weekly part of the worship service for all churches. However, whether it is included weekly or less frequently, the Supper is a powerful sign of God's coming. The Christ, who with his disciples took the first supper, gave it meaning because he indeed was the one who had come from the Father. And when he told us to remember him whenever we ate the bread or drank from the cup, he meant that we should do more than recollect his life on earth. He was helping us to see that he would come over and over again to us if we would be sensitive to the signs and be ready to receive him.

The sermon also is a way of God coming to us; he comes to us through word. The preacher is in the highest sense a translator of God's word to us. And the full symphony of worship is completed when the sermon becomes a translation of God's word and is heard. The sermon which truly helps persons to live out of faith is the kind that completes the worship experience. When the sermon is merely a discourse of personal opinion intended to tell people what the preacher wants them to hear, it cannot bear such a high purpose. It becomes merely a person's word to other persons, and that will not sustain either worship or real life.

Much sermonizing is an example of such discourse. A healthier approach is seen in what John Claypool would say prior to a sermon, "This sermon is God's word as it came to me. Perhaps it can also become the word of God to you." But somehow in the course of time, through preaching—the distorted and the healthy—the word comes through. Let us hope that the worshipers who participate with us will hear and obey.

The materials in this book, however, are not about the movement of God to us. I will leave that to others who have, on a regular basis, offered the Supper and the sermon to the worshiping congregation. My experience has been more with the part of worship which I have called our movement toward God: the call to worship, the invocation, the pastoral and confessional prayer, offertory prayers and sentences, and readings and litanies. In addition, I have included sections on Christmas, Easter, and Pentecost as well as some outlines of entire worship services. Most of the examples which I cite for these elements of worship were written as I participated in worship leadership at the Crescent Hill Baptist Church in Louisville, Kentucky. I also developed some of the materials for worship at the Midwestern Baptist Theological Seminary and the Englewood Baptist Church in Kansas City, Missouri.

I hope that this gift which I bring will help others approach more seriously the task of preparing worship materials. For if worship is what we say—a movement of worshiper to God and God to worshiper—then its preparation deserves our best thinking and our deepest sensing. With right thinking and sensitivity, worship leaders can see to it that worship is for all, not just for them, and they will resist the temptation to relegate the role of the congregation to that of watching them worship.

Chapter 1

Spoken Calls to Worship

The call to worship is literally an invitation to participate in worship. Along with the prelude, it has a tone-setting function. Its purpose, however, is broader than merely setting a tone for worship. That purpose is varied, and it is essential that you know it when you are writing a call.

Establishing a Motif

Sometimes the call establishes the motif for the service. When writing this kind of call, you should spend some time either with the primary planners of worship or with a copy of the order of worship. When I was asked to prepare the call to worship, the minister of music would sometimes tell me the kind of service he and the pastor were planning. Always he made a copy of the service available to me. He would suggest impressionistically what he had in mind for a call.

Once in a service that included the celebration of baptism and Communion, I called the congregation to worship with these words:

Worship is a banquet. God is the host. You are the guests. We who stand before you are the waiters. Therefore, as each delicacy is laid before you, let none of you fast. But let each feast and be filled upon what God provides.

The following call is reminiscent of Kierkegaard's belief that worship is drama. It is a call which grew out of the Danish philosopher's fresh insight into worship.

Worship is a drama. You are the actors. We are your prompters. God, himself, is the audience. Let the play begin, for God waits eagerly.

A Call from the World

The call may be built upon the notion of turning from the demands of the world to worship. It can come out of your feeling for how worship helps you to get in touch with the holy and transcendent. Care has to be taken not to leave the impression that what happens in worship is an escape from the world.

> Come, ye people. Come with your burdens, for this is a place of strength. Come with your joys, for this is a house of celebration.

The reminder of God's holiness does not have to be tied to the suggestion of turning from the world. It can stand on its own.

> Come.
> Come to worship.
> Come to worship God, the Holy One.

Here is another example, taken from an Advent service.

> Some things which for the moment seem important
> will in the annals of history make little difference.
> Our lives are filled with such experiences.
> But this makes the ultimate difference:
> the Christ has come and still comes.

A Call for Celebration

The theme of celebration is nearly always an appropriate one. To write a call to celebration requires that we actually see worship as a moving, living kind of activity. If we have known such moments of awareness and presence, we can, with little thought, shape a call that the congregation will hear as a genuine expression and will respond to positively.

> Sing when you think of God.
> Come, let us fill his house with loud thanksgiving.

This call from an Advent service contains a similar note.

> Bad news travels on swift wings. But good news is more welcomed. Here is some good news: The Christ has come and still comes. Let us find the meaning of that and celebrate its joy.

Here is a call with variations on Psalm 100.

Minister: The Lord is good.
Congregation: Praise God for his goodness.
Minister: His mercy is everlasting.
Congregation: Praise God for his mercy.
Minister: His Truth endures forever.
Congregation: Praise God for his Truth.
Minister: In his goodness he made us
Congregation: And called us to be his people.
Minister: In his mercy he came to us
Congregation: And forgave our transgressions.
Minister: In Christ he showed us Truth
Congregation: And made us free. And made us free.

A Call from Nature

That which is happening with nature and the changing seasons may suggest a call to worship. In the spring, autumn, and after a snowfall, people have these phenomena on their minds. If you walk with nature, this kind of call will easily come to you as you reflect on what you have seen during the day or week and attempt to put your feeling into a succinct word.

Outside, the dead leaves of winter are pushed back and the shoots of spring appear. It can be that way with worship. If we will push back the deadness of our existence, we will experience the energy of God.

● ● ●

The sun gilds the edges of the morning, and the world is transformed before our eyes. In worship, God touches the core of our being, and we are changed. Let us now prepare for his touch.

A Special Happening

The call to worship may reflect a national or regional event. It may deal with some special church event, such as the first Sunday of a revival. The calendar is nearly always a source of ideas for calls to worship. The following call to worship could have come simply from a calendar review, although in this case it was also influenced by the title of the pastor's sermon, "True Patriotism." This particular call also illustrates a certain restraint. Notice that the theme is citizenship and that the call hints at the motif of the service, but the call does not directly explain that a service on citizenship is beginning.

Come, you people of God.
Come, you children of Abraham.
Come to worship.
Come to worship him whose kingdom is forever.

The following call could be used on the Sunday before a national election:

This is a significant week in our national life.
We have decisions to make. Much is at stake.
What we do here in worship can give us
  perspective.
Come, then, pray, listen, and ponder.

On some occasions, rare ones, a longer call to worship may be used. This might be done to begin Holy Week services or a series of revival meetings. Preparation of such a call will, as you can see, involve more thought than the usual, brief, pithy calls. It may be written in a poetic style. However, it does not have to be poetic. It can be an excellent interpretive introduction to a special event, without the slightest trace of rhyme or rhythm.

I wrote the following call one Sunday afternoon for use in a Sunday evening Advent service. In other years it was used as a call to introduce the Advent season.

There was love here,
  but much of lovelessness,
And he came.
There was truth here,
  but much of error,
And he came.
There was light here,
  but much of obscurity,
And he came.
There was God here,
  but much of inaccessibility,
And he came.
There were sonship and daughtership here,
  but much of alienation,
And he came.

And because he came,
Love was rekindled in the ashes of anger;
Truth surged in error's den;

Light began pushing back the darkness;
God passed within reach;
And we who were already sons and daughters
received the power to become
the redeemed children of God.

God Meets Us

The belief that God meets us in worship is an engaging one. Regardless of the kind of service you are calling the congregation to participate in, this meeting with God can be expressed. A part of the strength of this belief is that it dispels the notion that God sits like an unemotional monarch on a throne and that we bow and scrape before him waiting for the scepter to fall either in favor or in disapproval.

For one service where the divine-human encounter was the theme, I wrote the call. My use of "meeting" was my own toning down of "encounter" and an expression of my profound conviction that there is a mutuality in worship in which we and God both hear and speak.

This is the place of meeting, where God moves
toward us. And we together reach for him.
It is a time to remember our covenant with him.
It is a time to confess and to rejoice.
We are here. He is coming toward us.
It is a happening.
Welcome to the meeting.

A Call from the News

The news of the week is another source for a call to worship. When we truly sense the ambiguities of some of these events and feel the tragedy which is inherent in them, we can find a call to worship that will help others. Of course, in these cases the idea is to suggest that the activity of worship will have some bearing on how we think and feel about such happenings and will remind us, as the last line of the following call does, of what Ethelbert Stauffer termed "the priority of the Divine."

The times are perilous.
They move as the ocean's shifting sands.
But do not despair.
Come here.
Exchange your drunken helplessness for sober
    cheer.

Fear not the day's demands.
Come, commune with him
who holds the times in his hands.

The newspapers, during a recent Christmas, carried a story about the possibility of the star of Bethlehem reappearing. As I read the article, I was impressed with the absence of any religious meaning as it talked about the star. The following call came out of this experience.

Yesterday's newspaper suggested the strong possibility that the star of Bethlehem would reappear in the future. The article was filled with scientific language about the phenomenon. There was no word about the meaning of the star. But we know that meaning here, for in the flame of the Advent candle is seen the meaning. The Christ has come and still comes.

The next call combines two kinds of calls to worship—the one from nature and the one from the nature of the times in which we live. I delivered it on the morning after an ice storm.

Much in this life is as uncertain as our footing on the ice. But this, this is for sure: The Christ has come and still comes.

On Worship

The call may define worship. At such times care should be taken not to get too involved or be verbose. The earlier call about worship being a banquet (see page 17) is an example of this kind of call. And the following is a bit more defining in a categorical sense.

Worship is as fresh as the spring rains. And when it is honest, it is, as the spring, both turbulent and beautiful. Worship here is that way. Therefore, the call to worship is the call to the reexamination of our attitudes, our emotions, and our actions. It is a call to see the worst of sin and the best of creation in us. Let us worship.

Another example is based on observations made in this book's Introduction.

Worship is a symphony with two movements.
We move toward God.
He moves toward us.
As these two join in divine and human harmony,
may we revel in worship's beauty and be inspired
by its meaning.

A call may take the form of a reading involving the minister and the congregation or several persons and groups. Later in the book I discuss such readings—or as they are called by some, litanies—but in connection with the call to worship I would like to point out that the best readings are made of brief sentences. I developed this one for vacation Bible school, and our minister of music sometimes chooses it for Sunday morning.

Minister: Good morning.
People: Good morning.
Minister: Who are you?
People: We are the people of God.
Minister: Who made you?
People: God, our Father, made us.
Minister: Where do you live?
People: We live in the Father's world.
Minister: Why are you here?
People: We are here to worship.
Minister: Let the worship begin.

Paraphrasing the Bible

The paraphrasing of Scripture provides an endless source of calls to worship. Actually "paraphrasing" may be too strong a word. What you do is write an impressionistic piece from your memory of a Bible verse or passage. You may, of course, go to the Bible and read the verse, but the tendency will be to attempt to stay too close to the words of the Scriptures. If you are going to do that, you might as well go ahead and quote the Scripture as the call to worship, which is, by the way, a very good kind of call. The material in the Psalms and the Prophets is especially useful; so are the sayings of Jesus and verses from the epistles.

The following two calls are examples of calls I wrote from my memory of two Bible passages.

Holy, holy, holy is the Lord.
The whole earth is full of his glory.
Let us worship him.

● ● ●

Send your joy toward God, everybody.
Serve him with gladness.
Come, singing.
Show your gratitude.

Bless God's name,
for he is good;
his mercy is everlasting,
and his truth endures.

Summary

In summary, what can be said about writing a call to worship? First, ask, "What is its purpose?" Does it suggest a motif; is it a call from the world; does it focus on God's holiness, call us to celebration, promise perspective for some future event, define the worship act, call persons to a meeting with God? As I hope we have shown, the answer to this question will determine the shape of the call.

Second, the call should be brief, although there will be special times when a longer call will be desirable. We might learn a lesson from television at this point. Notice how brief some very substantive promotional pieces and show introductions are.

Third, the call needs a certain reserve. I realize that this suggestion reflects my own approach. But it seems to me that if we are not careful, the call will preempt the invocation or other prayers and may even become a sermonette.

Fourth, the call may take poetic form. Rhyme, of course, is not necessary, but a call with some rhythm has a special flavor. This rhythm is not as difficult to obtain as one might think. Writing short sentences will help you get into a rhythm. Take, for example, a call built around a favorite Bible verse, John 3:16. Instead of giving it as one long sentence, attempt short ones.

God loves.
God loves the world.
God loves enough to give.
God loves the world enough to give his Son.
If we believe, we will have life.
Come, let us believe and receive.

Notice that I have changed "love" from the past tense to the present. This will cause some to hear the word who maybe have not listened for a while. Here is another call that utilizes a change of tense and the short statement.

The Christ has come.
And still comes.
As he comes to us today,
let us learn from him the meaning of his coming
and worship God as he did.

An Exercise in Writing a Call

Having said all of this about the call to worship, let us work on an exercise. We are going to prepare a call.

We are asked to write a call to worship for the service on Pentecost Sunday. Already we have a clue about direction for the call, and it is, of course, that we are dealing with a special day of the church year—Pentecost. But we move further in our preparation by finding out what the sermon is going to be about. And we learn that the topic is "The Power of Pentecost."

By this time we are ready to write down some words and phrases. I wrote:

> power . . . energy . . . the energy of God . . . dove . . .
> Holy Spirit . . . Spirit of God . . . Unseen God who is
> felt . . . wind . . . breath . . . our faith in the mate-
> rial . . . our uncertainty about the unseen
> . . . fire . . . cleansing . . . chaff . . . the hymn lines:
> "The flame shall not hurt thee; I only design thy dross
> to consume, and thy gold to refine"[1]. . .

It took me about five minutes to do the above. You can see that if you give at least fifteen minutes to such thought, you will find enough leads for writing a call to worship.

Remembering that the call is to be brief, is not to compete with the sermon, and may take a poetic form, how will you write it? I wrote:

> God moves by like wind and fire.
> The fire burns the dross from our lives.
> The wind blows away the chaff.
> In our worship on this Pentecost Sunday
> may we be refined by the fire and cleansed by
> the wind.

Taking another look at my clues, I wrote:

> We easily put our faith in the material
> but are uncertain about the unseen.
> Pentecost reminds us that the greatest power
> cannot be held in our hands or seen with our eyes.
> Come, let us experience this unseen energy,
> as we worship God.

Chapter 2

Invocations

The first prayer of the worship service is called the invocation. Its purpose is inherent in its label which means to ask for God's presence and aid. God is, of course, present whether we ask or not, and the invocation has a certain character that is supposed to help the worshiper to "live into" the service. The form the prayer assumes will depend upon what it is you want people to "live into."

Often the invocation is followed by the Lord's Prayer. The examples of such prayers are interspersed throughout this discussion of invocations.

God Meeting Us

The notion of dialogue and meeting, appropriate for the call to worship, may also shape the invocation. In such a prayer the ingredients are that both parties—we and God—need to say something and be heard and that we need to listen and really hear. In writing this kind of prayer, we need only to feel the deep desire we have to speak to God and to have God speak back, or to hear God's word as God comes to us and then to make some reply.

> As we gather in body and mind to worship, so do we gather in need and emotion, to speak and be spoken to, to hear and respond. We ask, O God, that you, out of your resources, meet us where we are, hear us and reply.

● ● ●

No temple can contain you; yet you meet us here if we come sincerely. God, reward our sensitivity to your presence as we pray, Our Father. . . .

On Worship

A similar theme is why we have come to worship and what there is for us in the worship experience. This kind of prayer can come easily out of worship experiences in which we have had some real need met. Doubtless you have sat in worship, singing a hymn which spoke to some feeling you had brought with you to the service. Did you not at such a time think to yourself, "That's right"? How many times has this line from the hymn "Immortal, Invisible, God Only Wise" spoken to persons who have had friends or relatives die: "We blossom and flourish as leaves on the tree, and wither and perish, but naught changeth thee"!

> Dear God, we come with our burdens to the house of strength. We come with our joys to the house of celebration. We come with our humanity to experience something of divinity. Help us with our desires as we pray the prayer of him who showed us both the human and the divine. . . .

The invocation may also be built around the elements of the worship service. This simply requires some thought about how the worship is put together. This can be especially valuable for the worshiper who, though regular in attendance and participative when present, does not think much about the form of worship.

> O God of grace and God of glory,
> Hear us as we praise Thee in prayer, in song, in lesson, and in word. In this hour of worship fill us with all Christlike graces and show us your glory. Hear us, thy children, as we pray. . . .

Doubtless you noted also that the above prayer draws from Fosdick's great hymn, which is another way to construct an invocation. The same can be done with Luther's hymn and others that make up our legacy of hymnody.

Recognizing God, the Source

The invocation may focus on God himself. This kind of prayer is especially corrective to worship which tends to be centered in the personalities of the worship leaders or which is too activistic. The prayer is a reminder of sources, that is, of Source.

> O Thou, out of whose creativity we were created,
> We live out of your life;
> We work out of your energy;

We experience transcendence because of your
  ongoingness;
And we worship here because in your initiative
you were here before we were.

Invocations of Praise

When the prayer focuses on God, it may take the form of praise. Such a prayer reveals some high moments in our lives when we were caught up in gratitude. You might say that these are the peak experiences written about by Abraham Maslow. They are also reminiscent of psalmic material.

O holy God, if in awe our lips were made silent, our hearts would pulsate with praise. And if our voices break forth in song, it is but the overflow of hearts filled with wonder. Before the wonder of being, we stand—sometimes mute, sometimes exuberant, sometimes in prayer. Hear us as we speak to Thee in silence, in praise, and in the prayer of our Lord. . . .

Invocations from Nature

This same kind of praise may be joined with an inspiration from nature to give added emphasis to God's creative activity.

O God, you are worthy of all praise. There is no God beside you. Since we can remember, you have brought the spring from winter's lair. And this year you have done it again. You have earth and heaven made. You have in your own image each of us made. And out of your energy we are given a new day of experience. There is no God beside you, O God. You are worthy of all praise. As we approach you in worship, we ask you to meet us at the place of our need. Hear the prayer of our Lord, who prayed, saying. . . .

C. S. Lewis told us that God did not need to be fawned over. Prayers of praise are not meant to be that but are intended to acknowledge something that we cannot keep hidden.

God's Nature

The focus on God can take another turn. The prayer can be Trinitarian in nature, or it can build around certain modes by which God expresses himself. When you think about this—Father, Son, Holy Spirit; mercy, justice, love; all-knowing, ever-present; Creator,

Sustainer, End—you can see the endless wealth of resources for such a prayer.

O ever-present God,
make yourself known here today.
O all-knowing One,
instruct us with wisdom.

O God of mercy,
forgive our sins.
O God of love,
surround us with your care
As we worship you.

Invocations at Special Events

The attributes of God can also be included in a prayer that comes on a Sunday after a special holy day, such as Christmas. Its purpose is to summarize the meaning of the event, to express its significance. Since many worshipers tend to forget, like daily headlines, the religious epochs of the year, it falls to us who lead worship to prod such short memories. An invocation can be especially helpful here, for it can, without preaching, simply utilize some words and phrases that will awaken within the worshiper the realization that something significant which happened only recently had almost been forgotten, but now is remembered.

O divine Presence
whose fullness emptied the tomb;
O great Creator whose touch brought life from
    death;
O Father
whose love would not forsake forever a Son;
We pray to Thee the prayer the devoted Son taught
    us. . . .

Here is another prayer in the same vein; it does not include reference to the Trinity or characteristics of God but is a reflection of a past event. This one also includes a spark of the pastoral, for it assumes that worshipers have looked at the meaning of Christmas on the one hand and the real world on the other.

As when the morning clouds hide the dawn we are tempted
to say the new day is not coming, so when the clouds of this
world obscure the Christmas event, we say the Light did not

come. But, alas, O God, even from behind the clouds the
Light is all around, pushing back the darkness. And the
Light of Christmas shines and the darkness is not putting it
out. Oh, Light, illumine this hour of worship.

There are a few times, very few, when the invocation needs to be
longer than usual. This is true especially when there is no pastoral
prayer in the service. Some Christmas services or Holy Week services
or preaching mission services will not include a pastoral prayer. The
invocation can fill both roles. The word used to describe the approach
to such a prayer is "reserve." This word seems to be a favorite of mine,
but it is, I think, a quality in the writer which gives quality to the
prayers. Such praying approaches thoughts which well deserve full
sermons, but it is not the time or place to deliver them. Thus, the
thought is to be tossed out and left to the listener to take more deeply
and farther. Here is a Maundy Thursday invocation.

Dear God,
We would want always to stand before the cross as a
reminder of how far you will go with your love, and how far
we will go with our hate. But every year at this Maundy
celebration we attempt to be there in a more intense way.
And so, here we are, with our shoes off, on holy ground. As
we stand here, in a sense with the whole world, in another
sense alone, we pray for engagement. We know that we
cannot taste the dust from the road, or hear the clamor of
the curious, or see the eyes of the empathetic. But through
word, faithfully recorded and passed on, and through
music, created under inspiration, we can hear and be
engaged.
We are listening, O God; engage us.
We pray in the name of the One being crucified.

And the following one was offered on the evening of the
trimming of the Chrismon tree at Christmas and the musical
presentations by the children's choirs. This prayer came just after the
singing of "Joy to the World."

God,
Our songs of joy and peace must sound strange to a world
that is wracked by war and despair, and our affirmation of
truth must ring hollow to those who are the victims of
deceit. Yes, there are places where the joy is muted and the
peace gone. Still the church sings, not because we think

you're in your heaven and all's right with the world, but because we believe that in Bethlehem the kingdom was begun and that it is still coming. Help us to remember that we are witnesses to an event that is coming right now, not just to one of long ago. Honor our affirmations that this holy season means that you have heard our cries and that you are acting to bring this earth to a reign of truth and peace.

Invocations Dealing with Personal Feelings

The feelings of the worshiper form another focus for the invocation. In such cases the worship leader has to resist the temptation to make the invocation into a pastoral prayer. This can be done by approaching but not moving deeply into the assumed feelings of the congregation.

O God,
Our utterances do not always show forth thy
     praise,
because we stand
between clarity and confusion,
between love and indifference,
between commitment and withdrawal,
between righteousness and sin.
We are here in this place because we want to
     rid ourselves of that which hinders our praise of
     thee.
Help us as we pray. . . .

Again, as with the call to worship, the invocation may hint that the service of worship has something to do with the past week and the week ahead. This does not have to be built around a special religious day or even a nonreligious day but merely around the fact that every week is one of experience. That experience has meaning—if we can only find it. Worship is a place where it might be found.

Dear God,
Our hearts we lift to you in thanksgiving that you have brought us to this good hour. May it be an hour in which we find the meaning of what has happened to us during the past week and perspective for decisions we will face during the week ahead. We are here for worship and praise. Hear us as we pray. . . .

Sometimes the invocation will come out of your experience, and the congregation will have no idea of the source. Never mind, a prayer can have meaning without the congregation knowing the full background. What has to be avoided in this kind of prayer, however, is the hidden agenda element which more nearly approaches an off-the-chest exercise than real prayer. The following prayer came from thinking about the importance of having a vital Christian experience before we attempt to witness to others.

O God who made us, O God who sustains us, help us to know that we cannot lead others to see that they are your children unless first we become convinced of our own sonship and daughtership. Help us to know that we cannot do for others unless first we are somebody. We are your children, and we are here to worship.

Summary

What, in summary, can be said about writing an invocation? Keep a distinction between this prayer and the pastoral or morning prayer. Shape the invocation according to the purpose it is to serve. In most cases it will be a very brief prayer. Its thoughts are to be concise and not followed up on in any depth. These thoughts might appear later in more depth in the pastoral prayer or the sermon or in some other element in the service.

One final hint is, perhaps, appropriate. The number one hindrance to better prayers is the use of the same phrases over and over—clichés, as they say. A deacon who meant much to me as I was growing up in my home church always began his prayers with the phrase "Kind and merciful heavenly Father." This posed no problem with his being heard, for I suspect that God heard this man's prayers with delight. But in terms of form, the phrase would have had more meaning if reserved for prayers that were going to deal with God's kindness and mercy.

But are the prayers in this chapter spontaneous? some will ask. They are, in the sense that they were written for special times and services. They are not suggested as a kind of common prayer. They are mere illustrations of different kinds of prayers. Your own prayer—written or unwritten—will be spontaneous.

Chapter 3

Pastoral Prayers

The pastoral prayer carries a heavy burden in worship. I learned this from Othar Smith, at Bowling Green, Kentucky, whose prayers took us to the "throne of grace." As in Communion and baptism, the minister is exercising a priestly role in this prayer. Such a prayer will take many forms and be delivered in many different styles. Regardless, it is essentially the gathering of some major concerns of the worshiping congregation and offering these to God. Not every concern of every person can be included, or else the prayer would be too long and essentially the same each week. The sensitive minister will know which wrenchings, which ambiguities, which sins the worshipers bring to the service. And the pastoral prayer will be built around these.

I was tempted, and probably sometimes have succumbed, to use the pastoral prayer as a brief sermon. I have heard morning prayers which were previews of the sermon. At other times they were actually sermons. This violates both the prayer and the sermon, for it distorts one and detracts from the other.

The reason the pastoral prayer is not a sermon is that it is supposed to show the priestly minister catching up the thought and feeling of the congregation and turning with these to God. A sermon is just the opposite. It is directed toward the congregation and may indeed become the word from God.

Pastoral prayers come from experience. They require much thought if they are to be meaningful and not too long. I invest from one to two hours in the preparation of these prayers. Starting with the worship bulletin, I examine every element of the worship service, often reading some of the Scriptures and hymn texts. Then I immerse myself in thought, reflecting on the week behind, anticipating the one ahead, looking for the significance of the Sunday on which the prayer is to be offered. I write down brief phrases and thoughts. Eventually the prayer comes to me, and I write it down.

Prayer for the New Year

Special times of the year are also special times of the soul. We face these times with joy and fear. Looking back upon our lives, we face them. And looking ahead into the unknown, we face them. We seldom verbalize this tension, but in any thinking person it is present and real. Birthdays, New Year's Day, and Christmas are such times when the worshipers come to the service with this backward-forward experience. An effective pastoral prayer will attempt to summarize these feelings and put them in some kind of perspective. The following prayer was offered on the first Sunday of a new year. It does not attempt to review the year; that task is for sermons and newspaper editorials. But the prayer does capture something of a theme that ran through the life of our church during the year.

O God of the old and of the new; O God of the age and of the ages; O God who in mercy forgives and in hope calls us into the not-yet.

As we enter upon a new year's pilgrimage, we are filled with mixed feelings. Like shackles upon our limbs, our guilt binds us. Like cataracts over our eyes, our fears blind us to the life that is before us.

In looking back over the year that is gone, the audit shows imperfection and sin. We have deceived. We have cheated. We have been selfish. We have hurt. We have made gods of silver and of prestige. We have amassed goods while much of the world has struggled to survive.

Much of this we have done willfully; but intermittently we have seen higher visions of who we are. Deep inside we have known that our defection is not the first or the last word about who we are. We have heard the good news that the first word about us is that in your image we have been made. And however faintly, that word has begun to be heard and is shaping how we feel about ourselves, how we relate to others, and how we relate to you.

We confess, here before the new gate, that we have sinned. And we ask you to forgive us and to help us hear in clearer tones that first word about our true nature.

If, O God, you can forgive us for sin and can remove our burdening guilt, cannot you also allay our fears for the new that is before us? Too many scenes of war and hunger haunt us from yesterday for us to be cavalier about tomorrow.

But alongside that good word about our worth in your sight are those surges of hope about the not-yet. And that is partly why we are here today—to receive out of the church's post-Christmas life some word to steady us and to challenge us as we enter upon the new year's journey.

As we wait before your word, O God, will you speak the freeing word.

Amen.

A Prayer in Spring

Spring has always been a time when I experience the exhilaration of new life as what seems dead comes to life and what seems hopeless becomes possible. If you are a child of the spring season, you, too, will find in it a message that no other season bears. Many worshipers have these same inner feelings but have not put them into words. A pastoral prayer springing from the season of life and hope will indeed be priestly. This prayer comes out of that kind of experience.

O creating God,
As the spring rains fall, so is thy mercy showered upon us; mercy that delivers us from the barren winters of our sin; mercy that flowers within us the signs of renewal; mercy that is never ceasing.

Sometimes thy mercy comes gently, as softly as this day's rain. Sometimes it comes thunderingly, with the convulsions of spring storms—not out of wrath on thy part, but because of the utter deadness of our situation. When the deep winters of our defection move, by thy mercy, toward renewal, we cannot but expect the travail that comes.

O God, we know that thy image within us is obscured by our unresponsiveness to life. We have chosen to eat of the tree that brings only unfaith. We have doubted the goodness of creation. We have rejected life for an imprisonment either within the confines of our deadening rules or within the undisciplined life that neither feels nor acts with any sensitivity.

As the spring rains fall, dear God, deliver us from the colorless life to the intended life of fragrance and beauty. Free us for the abundant life of thine intention for us. And as thy mercy comes to us without price, may we pass it on to others, replacing our inhumanity with acts of divinelike love. Our barren world needs the flowering of renewal. Dear God, use us to help it happen, just as the spring rains fall and the earth once again comes to life.

Amen.

A Prayer out of Pain

Sometimes the pastoral prayer comes out of a happening in the life of the congregation, a happening so pervasive as to shape the entire Sunday experience of a church. Such was the case in my church when in a Saturday's twilight Laura Lue Claypool, the little daughter of our pastor's family, lost her struggle with leukemia. During the long months she had suffered with the disease, the congregation had lived with the tension between hoping she would be well again and the sad facts of the course the disease was taking. The Sunday after her death, I was scheduled to give the pastoral prayer. How was I to gather up this event and lead the congregation to God with it? The prayer was not to be a sermon on death or life. And I would not allow it to be a deliberate time for manipulating emotions that were at their peak.

I don't remember how many hours I waited for some clear way of putting together a prayer for this awful day. But eventually it came, and a vision of a God of light, mercy, and hope was before me. I wanted that same vision to be before the congregation on the morrow. This brief prayer was such an attempt.

> O God of light,
> the miracle we had so longed
> for has not been given,
> And we face with our friends
> a dark darkness.
> Nearly all of us, of sufficient
> years, have stood at the edge
> of darkness; and most of us
> have had to go in.
> We thank you that there is

with the night a commensurate
light to help us see our way.

O God of mercy,
You are infinite, we are finite,
And we do not understand
all your ways.
We pray that in your mercy
we might be given the grace
to live with your silence
And to accept even though
we do not understand.

O God of hope,
We sometimes live as if there
were nothing except what is,
And therefore we despair.
Teach us that what seems to
be is not always what is,
that in the most desperate
of times, there is yet the
occasion for hope.

Above the pain of separation
remind us again that to
be born into this time is
to become and to enter
into eternal possibilities
with you, that the veil
of death is indeed not the end.

O very God,
Lead us through this night;
lift up our burden with
your strong right arm;
in your compassion help
us to bear this unbearable
sorrow; give us to see that
the darkness of our
night will be turned
into morning, that the
winter of our grief will
give way to the
resurrection of spring.

O God of light,
O God of mercy,
O God of hope,
O very God,
We are bowed down;
help us up.

Amen.

A Prayer of Repentance and Gratitude

The next prayer carried two duties. It did what the previous prayer did—spoke to an event in the life of the church which was on everyone's mind. It also spoke to an event in the life of the nation. Thus, in addition to being sensitive to what the entire church was thinking about, it also responded to a national happening. Current events are another source for the pastoral prayer. These national crises, of course, happen with such rapidity that each clamors to push the other from the front page. Whatever the happening, people will be having strong and sometimes confused feelings about it. A pastoral prayer can help the worshipers work through those feelings.

This particular prayer was given the Sunday after the terrible Attica uprising. The event could not be ignored. Equally pregnant in the day was the fact that it also was the last Sunday for our pastor before he moved on to another congregation. The two themes were inseparable because this minister had repeatedly called us to a high social consciousness.

O God, Father of us all, all week we have, in our thought, been turning to Attica and asking whether it is so far from heaven that you didn't know what was happening, or whether you were depending upon us to represent you in that situation of rage and irrationality. If that place is so far from nowhere that even you didn't know, then we are in a hopeless and absurd world, and there are no voices by which we can shape our despair. If you were depending upon us, we ask for forgiveness, for like at Rome, Auschwitz, and Hiroshima, like at My Lai, Selma, and Belfast, we forgot that we are brothers and sisters all; that under you there is no black or white, Catholic or Protestant, inmate or guard. We all dehumanize. We all are guilty, and we need your help.

O God of gifts, there's no way to pray today about the world without acknowledging the good gift of our brother and spiritual leader for this past decade.

We thank you for the vision of personhood that he has given us—that it is sheer gift to be celebrated and lived redemptively, that though we should most often want to soar as the eagle, or at least to run, there are times when our greatest need is the strength merely to walk and not to faint; that though we want security, there are times when we will be called upon to make our beds in hell; that in the face of the screams of frustration and disillusionment, we are to be the children of reconciliation.

We thank you for the vision of you, the Father, that he has shown us—that you have power but give freedom; that you have authority but show love; that you pass judgment but far prefer mercy; and that you delight in us your sons and daughters more than in the stars that light the darkened abyss of night, and that you expect of us a certain nobility that astonishes the world.

We pray for him and for us, that we might be, hereafter, in our separate spheres of influence, true brothers and sisters of our elder, Jesus, and true sons and daughters of yours, our Father. Amen.

Praise in Spite of Pain

There will be times when the pastoral prayer will be intensely personal. It will come almost entirely from your own experience, although most likely some others in the congregation will be aware of what is happening. This is the kind of prayer I delivered on an August Sunday morning, several weeks after the death of our own daughter, Laura. It was my first Sunday back in the worship leader role. As I was thinking about this prayer, what came to me was a prayer of praise for blessings and praise in spite of pain. It is a prayer all of us can pray who have known high joy and unbearable sadness.

"Mighty God, while angels bless Thee,
May a mortal sing thy name?"[1]
You are worthy of all praise, O God.
The cherubim play at your feet,
and the seraphim sing around your head.
And we mortals attempt with stammering songs
to praise you.

Some praise you from a
life of unbroken good fortune.
All has been well with them,
and all that their hands have touched
has succeeded and multiplied.
They want to thank you.

Others praise you
from the ruins of shattered dreams,
and from their disappointments
with ambition and power
there is still a song for you.

Some praise you
from the darkness of facing the uncertain
    future.
In faith they accept their inability
to plot the future or to stay
the heady winds of fate.
And they have a song for you.

Others voice praise alongside the anger
of facing haughty death
as she stalks the earth
defying the power of love to hold.
And against the irrational
we take our deep breaths
and sing a song to you.

We all praise you that beyond the obscuring
    clouds,
there is light;
that beyond the rumbles of thunder,
there is laughter in the spheres;
that against the seemingly absurd,
there is a wisdom holding the universe together;
that against the devastating powers of the demonic,
there is a center that holds. Amen.

A Prayer of Repentance

The pastoral prayer may be a kind of "entering prayer" for a special religious season. This kind of prayer comes from thinking through the activities of the event and anticipating some of the feelings the worshipers will bring to it. Once I was assigned the pastoral prayer for the Sunday before Lent. In our theological tradition we have not made much of such celebrations; thus we have entered upon Easter unprepared and have had no depths against which to put the joy of resurrection. As I thought of this missing dimension, I shaped this prayer.

> Dear God, soon Easter will be here and we will clap our hands with the news that our Lord has been resurrected after death. But we shall miss the greater joy unless we also come forth from death. Help us, then, during this Lenten time to assume, even as our Lord did, our own appropriate fast, so that we may come to the day of resurrection to find the new life that comes from sacrifice.

> We are not accustomed either to serious preparation or to sacrifice. And perhaps that is why we lack the joy of resurrection. Take away our shallow experience whereby we assume false crowns that have come from no crosses. So, O God, lead us during this season in sacrificial and somber preparation for the trials of Holy Week that we may move, though with agony and hurt, toward the day of renewal. While we think of fasting, we are also reminded that there are some things we need to add to our experience.

> We have not loved as we should. Some of us have not shown the proper love for our families. Children have, in selfishness, disobeyed. Young people have, in ingratitude, deprived parents of satisfaction; and parents have, in insecurity, robbed children of self-determination.

> Forgive us.

> Some who have sufficiently loved their own have not been as concerned for others outside the family circle. "Me and mine" for too long has controlled our attitude about the needs of others.

> Forgive us.

> Some who have loved others have done so only to the lovely. Help us to love the unlovely and even those who hate us. If some in hatred draw circles that shut us out, give us the magnanimity of spirit to draw the larger circle of love that takes our enemies in.

> Is this not what Thou hast done, O God?

Our narrow vision of humanity had no room for the man Jesus; so we sought to put him away. But around our narrowness thou didst take us in. We stand before such love with gratitude and hope—gratitude to Thee and hope that we might become like him—beginning on this first Sunday of preparation for Easter. Amen.

Praise for Light

The pastoral prayer may be built around a central thought and, therefore, be indirectly pastoral. Formulating such a prayer requires more thought than one that focuses on concerns in the lives of the congregation. It comes from what Samuel Miller called "resonance,"[2] i.e., the interplay between faith and the experiences of life, between flesh and spirit, and between God and his world. Maybe, on a less grandiose scale, it is like what Handel said about the composition of the *Messiah:* "I did think I did see all Heaven before me, and the great God Himself!"[3]

O God within us,
but not imprisoned by our finiteness,
O God beyond us,
but not alien to our human situation,
you are the source of all that is praiseworthy,
and we praise you.

We praise you for your creating Spirit
that hovered over the primeval abyss
and wrested the light
from the pitch black of night.

We praise you for the sun's light
that chases the night
and beckons us to a new day.

We praise you for the light of reason
that frees us from our superstitions
and keeps us from the preys of ignorance.

We praise you for the light of beauty
that raises a yellow flower
in the window of the ghetto,
that bursts in a child's laughter,
that speaks in the wrinkles of age.

We praise you for the light of artistry

that turns ordinary words into poetry;
that holds together the strings, winds, and
  horns
to make a symphony.

We praise you for the light of courage
that will not forever let the human spirit
be driven like sand and leaves blown by the
  wind,
but which lifts us to full measure to declare,
"We are persons."

We praise you for the light of peace
that moves us in love toward those
who move toward us in hate,
that prods the human conscience
to cry out against the waste of war.

O God, we praise you for the light.
And though it is often as precarious
as a flickering candle flame,
we live in the hope that it will stay the
  darkness
and that ill winds will not snuff it out.

O kindly Light, lead us from within, from
  beyond.
Amen.

Gratitude for Music

Another example of this kind of prayer is one I prepared for a musical
program. Again, it has something of the poetic in it, and it speaks to a
single thought—music. Happily, in this case, it also coincided with a
significant evening in the life of the church when all of the choirs were
leading us in worship.

O Thou who dost play upon the sunbeams
as a musician upon the lyre,
O Thou who dost sing through the willows
and orchestrate through the driving wind and
  rain,
We thank you for the beauty of music—
the music of the spheres
and the music that artists find within them.

We thank you for music that soothes
and for that which awakens us;
for music to walk by,
music to run by,
and music by which we soar.
As shadows in the late afternoon
play upon the house and yard,
so have you given us music for reflection;
as birds signal the coming dawn
so have you given us music for stirring.
We thank you, O God of beauty,
for the gift of music
to accompany our days upon the earth.   Amen.

The Attributes of God

Still another approach to the pastoral prayer is to build it around
some attributes of God and the place where they meet our experience.
Some of the earlier prayers have this characteristic in them, but here
is one that was prepared deliberately after this model. The genesis of
such a prayer is in your own thinking about what God is like, how he
works, how he relates to us his creatures. As you work with this kind
of thinking as well as with what you know from human experience,
this kind of prayer will fall into shape.

O God of beauty, we have much to praise you for. Autumn
has shown her splendor, and the colors are beautiful. The
sun lights a yellow tree, and we turn aside to see such
marvelous work. Like Moses of old, we remove our shoes,
for we are overwhelmed.

The joy of human relations is before us—the affirming
child, the loving companion, the loyal friend, the helpful
colleague. For such moments and relationships we are
grateful, God of beauty.

O caring God, beside the beauty and the joy there is the
painful. Not all is well in our families or where we work.
There is alienation, bitterness, disappointment, and
conflict, and we need strength of spirit to hold on.

Will you help us as your children to move in these difficult
situations, that from them might come the redemption both
you and we want, O caring God?

O transcendent God, we need some perspective on national events. Like ancient peasantry we watch the royal court play its high-risk games and we are afraid. The happenings we see don't fit the rhetoric we hear, and we are confused. The gods we've made are fallible, and we feel betrayed.

Will you call from us and our leaders the noble and the good, that we might be delivered from this dark time?

O God of beauty,
    we praise you.
O caring God,
    stand beside us.
O transcendent God,
    speak to us.   Amen.

Prayer for All Ages

A pastoral prayer may acknowledge the age groups represented in the worshiping congregation. It is a seldom used way of expressing the beauties and tasks of growing up. This kind of prayer is not pastoral in an intercessory way but is pastoral in that it can reflect your identification with all members of your congregation. I once shaped a prayer like this and for several weeks church members came up to me to tell me of some experience that I had referred to in the prayer.

O God of all time
    and of every age,
O Father of all humankind
    and of every person,
O Spirit in the limitless space
    and in us,
We praise you for who you are
    and for what you are trying to make of us.
You are worthy of all praise.

We praise you for *childhood:*
the wonder of dripping faucets,
finding peculiar shaped rocks,
touching worms as they measure the sidewalk,
birds singing in the morning,
sounds of night after we go to bed,
throwing rocks in the lake,
picking wild flowers,
ice-cream cones dripping on our chins,

riding on Dad's shoulders,
listening to Mother read a story,
learning to ride a bicycle with training wheels,
   then without,
being able to cry when we are hurt,
being able to laugh when something is funny.

We praise you for *youthhood:*
an expanding world of people and places,
growing taller and developing,
becoming coordinated at last,
the noise of a transistor,
the quiet strings as they play a folk song,
uncritical friends who accept us,
teachers who equip us to function in our world,
parents who understand us,
places to hang out,
the touch of a friend's hand,
discipline of the arts and of sports.

We praise you for *adulthood:*
seeing the shades of blue on
deep waters dashed with sparkles from the sun,
hues of green on the tiered hills of eastern
   Kentucky,
the embrace of a faithful marriage mate,
the satisfaction of hard work,
the responsibility for providing a home, a
   church,
and the institutions of society,
hearing the uninhibited laughter of children
splashing in a swimming pool,
participating in the maturing
of energetic teenagers around us,
friends who are glad to see us.

Yes, O God, we praise you for
this life; and though there
are times when there is no song
on our lips because there is no
joy in our hearts, we thank you
for those joys that make us want
to sing every song we hear. Amen.

A Prayer out of Struggle

Earlier we talked about the intensely personal prayer. Another kind of prayer, very close to that, is one in which you bare your soul before the congregation. Such a prayer is not without its pastoral dimension, for it will be shared by many. Still it shows a certain personal, inner struggle. And since it comes at a particular moment in one's personal history, it will show what struggles are real. Some will say that the following prayer is cynical, or what Leslie Weatherhead's friend Lord Birkett would label as the prayer of a "Christian agnostic." However, it ends with an affirmation of faith. I did not tack the affirmation on. Rather, it was part and parcel of the struggle reflected in the lines of the prayer.

O God, we have learned from our fathers and from our own experience that you are a God of love and mercy, of order and beauty. And this knowledge has caused us to praise you.

At the same time that we sing your praise, we also admit our perplexity at the unevenness of our existence upon the earth. And we are confused as to what you let happen and what you personally arrange.

We know that it is the questing minds you have given us that have sent men to walk on the moon and to stay in space, but why must some persons crawl the dust of some parched land in search of food and water? How much of this kind of paradox have you simply let happen; how much have you arranged?

While some persons exult in the fulfillment of their careers, others find their work gone—either because of health or failure.

While some of our young people step eagerly into the day, finding the energy to laugh and play, others lie in the hospital, uncertain of what is ahead for them. Have you willed it, or has it just worked out that way?

While one family celebrates the joy of a baby at the house, another lives with the stares and hostilities of dissolution— as a family falls apart.

While one family revels in a life together, another stands in the darkness of death and is lonely and confused. Why this stark unevenness, O God? Perhaps it is futile for us even to ask. Like the star which we cannot reach, perhaps the answers we could not understand.

If this be the case, then our prayer is more for grace than for knowledge—grace to live with this universal unevenness: grace that when there is accomplishment and joy and new life and family togetherness, we may be present to it with all of our powers—a living ode to joy; grace that when there is failure, and sickness, conflict and death, we may have the strength of spirit to endure—a living ode to courage. If you will not tell us what just happens and what you personally arrange, at least hold us together when the worst befalls us, as you did for your Son, Jesus, when history closed in upon him.

We pray in his name.
Amen.

The Directed Prayer

A special form of the pastoral prayer is what is called the directed prayer. Such a prayer asks for participation from the congregation. It calls on worshipers to offer silent prayers. It may also include a brief prayer by the person who is leading this part of the service. It may be a simple prayer that invites members of the congregation to pray for certain needs, or it may take the form of confession, thanksgiving, intercession.

This prayer follows the form of confession, intercession, and praise.

Confession:

Were he of wood or stone, God would not hear us. Neither would he care that we groan, nor forgive us for our sin. Confess, then, to him the forms your defection has taken— those of thought, of speech, of activity.

You need not beg in your confession; merely acknowledge your awareness that wrong has been conceived, voiced, done. He will hear. . . .

As with his hearing, so with his mercy—he forgives. If you have truly confessed, he has surely heard, and you are forgiven.

Intercession:

Having experienced his mercy upon your sins, take to him the needs of others. Make your prayers of intercession at this time—

for problems in your family,
for needs in the church,
for problems where you work,
for needs in the nation and world.

Praise:

Now give your whole being to his praise. No one is like he is in mercy.

O God, there is no God besides thee. None other is like thee in mercy. The gods of wood and stone have not heard us, but thou hast received our confessions and forgiven our defection. Thou hast heard our intercessions. And we give our whole beings to thee in thanksgiving. Amen.

Confession alone may mark the directed prayer, as in the following:

To the congregation:

We all participate in a common defection from creation. It is a sin of our own choosing, but it is also one out of the momentum of the sin history of humankind. Through the grace of the Creator we are not left either without help for our personal defection or without a momentum of holiness concurrent with the momentum of sin. In the face of this kind of grace, let us confess our sin.

Then offer this prayer:

O You who comes walking in the cool of the day through the garden of our existence, we have been hiding because we couldn't face you. We had forgotten for a while that you loved us in spite of our sin. Now we have remembered your unqualified love; now we have told you of our sin; now we thank you for your merciful forgiveness. Amen.

Summary

Three words, in reflection, need to be said about the pastoral prayers. One, I address God as "You" and "Thou." I feel sure he doesn't mind which word we use. Either word is personal and at the same time recognizes who God is—the One who made us.

Two, these prayers are not the same as the conversational

prayers you will find in some books. They are not as informal as
Malcolm Boyd's; and while they recognize God as one who cares,
they do not sound like friend-to-friend talk. Neither are they what we
might call "closet" prayers. They are public prayers, formulated to
help a worshiping congregation look to God.

Three, the popular phrase "In Jesus' name" is missing. This,
however, does not mean that the prayers are not in his name. Indeed,
behind them is the grand truth that it is the life of the Christ which has
shown us a caring Father with whom we can talk. I do have prayers
which I have ended in the popular way, but this ending is not at all
required for the prayer to be sincere or heard or answered.

Exercise in Writing a Pastoral Prayer

Let us now write a pastoral prayer for the first Sunday of Advent.

The first clue for direction has been given. The prayer is to help
the worshipers begin moving into the Advent experience. But how?
we ask next. And in order to answer that question, we must stop, turn
our minds from distractions, and meditate.

First, write down some words and phrases that come to you as
you think and feel. I wrote:

> Christ . . . the Christ is coming . . . the Christ has come . . .
> (And because of previous experience) the Christ has come
> and still comes . . . celebration . . . Bethlehem . . . Nazareth
> . . . the commercial . . . the real meaning of Christ . . .
> ritual . . . bells . . . Christmas season . . . preparation . . .
> repentance . . . hope . . . peace . . . joy . . . singing . . . giving
> and receiving . . .

By giving about thirty minutes to this kind of activity, you will
write down more than enough words and phrases from which to
shape a prayer. If they are available, you might also talk with the
pastor and other worship leaders about the content of the various
Advent services.

Now, how shall we address God? Have you ever heard a prayer
that did not do that? I have, and it always leaves me with a feeling of
an unresolved chord in a musical piece. Besides, it is more polite to
give a name to the person we are addressing.

Some possibilities, from the above clues, are:

> Dear God of Christmas . . . O God of celebration (or
> celebrating God) . . . God, who comes to us . . . Dear
> giving God . . . O Thou who in the Christ has come and

who still comes . . . God of joy, God of peace, God of hope . . .

Next, follow your chosen address with what is on your heart.

Dear giving God, we thank thee for giving us Jesus Christ. And as we begin this season of celebrating his birth, help us . . . etc.

Or you might take the joy-peace-hope trilogy and make it into something like this:

O God of joy, we are here to celebrate with you and our friends the joy of the Advent season. We praise you for the delights which enrich our days. We pray for those whose lives are filled with sadness . . . etc.

O God of peace, we thank you for the Prince of Peace who has come to us. May his peace work through us to heal the warfare of our fractured world . . . etc.

O God of hope, speak to the despair which binds so much of this world which you love. May the Christ be seen in us, so that others may turn from their hopelessness and find a renewed zest for the life which you have given them . . . etc.

In an hour and a half or two, you should have a pastoral prayer that will truly bring your congregation into the spirit of the Advent.

Chapter 4

Offertory Prayers and Sentences

The act of giving is a significant and regular part of the worship service. In nearly every instance it is either preceded or followed by a prayer. The offertory prayer, as it is called, is a brief dedication prayer for the tithes and offerings the congregation brings. A brief prayer built around gifts and giving provides a clear focus on this part of worship. If the offering stands on its own as a legitimate act of worship, it will fit into the worship service. On the other hand, a long, rambling prayer will detract from the integrity of the act of giving and will convey to the congregation that the offering is not a vital part of the service.

Some churches add variety to this part of worship by utilizing the offertory sentence instead of the prayer. Obviously, it also should be brief and related to the act of giving and should be entered in the order of worship as an "offertory sentence" or "dedication sentence."

Offertory prayers and sentences may be written around several themes. One of my favorite themes is that of joy. It seems to me that prayers at the time of bringing the offering are too much tied to duty and guilt rather than to willingness and joy. This one line comes out of this concern.

Only he who gives with joy truly gives.

The idea of joy in giving can be linked with reference to the gift.

If you are to give, it must be with joy,
for the cheerless giver is no giver at all,
and the cheerless gift, no gift.

Our giving can be compared to God's giving. Note that the joy theme is here also.

Our gifts cannot match his.
But if given as he gave,
they are acceptable to him.
So give for the joy of it.

This same idea of comparing God's way of giving and our way is the approach of this next sentence.

A gift carries with it no stipulation;
It is an unencumbered offering.
This is the way God has given to us.
Let this be the way we give to him.

Here in a more rhythmic form is the same thought.

God, out of his goodness, gives to us.
We, out of our joy, give to him.
God, out of goodness to us.
We, out of joy to him.
God, out of goodness.
We, out of joy.

The notion of God as the source of gifts and we as stewards is another approach.

All things were made by him.
All things are his.
Let us be good stewards of his trust in us.

Sometimes the giving of money is viewed as the only expression of stewardship. At other times it seems unimportant because it is viewed as only one among many expressions. The following sentence speaks to these distortions.

The giving of money is no more important than stewardship
in other areas of life. Neither is it any less important. Give,
then, to the degree that you also give your mind, your
ability, your time.

The connection between stewardship of money and of self is in another form in this sentence.

True and worthy stewardship comes from a prior
commitment of self. May it be so of your gift today.

Here the gift is tied with praise.

It is a good thing to give thanks to the Lord. And it is a good thing to remember in stewardship all his gifts to us.

The offering sentence may come out of the previous hymn of worship. This next one came after the congregation had sung the Christmas carol "It Came upon the Midnight Clear." The unifying theme of the carol is singing angels. Here is the sentence I used to follow that hymn and precede the offering.

And what can we give for the angels' song but a song of our own in return, and with that song share what we have been given.

As with other elements of worship, a Scripture passage can form the offertory sentence.

But this I say, He which soweth sparingly shall reap also sparingly; and he which soweth bountifully shall reap also bountifully (2 Corinthians 9:6).

The sentence may be a verse from a hymn, such as:

Trust Me, try Me, prove Me,
saith the Lord of hosts, And see
if a blessing, unmeasured blessing,
I will not pour out on thee.[1]

The hymn may be in the form of a prayer.

We give thee but thine own,
whate'er the gift may be.
All that we have is thine alone,
A trust, O Lord, from thee.[2]

Or, the prayer may be inspired by the offertory hymn. For example, after the singing of "O for a Faith That Will Not Shrink," this prayer was used.

God, so many times the strength of our faith is challenged. We are called on to believe in times of doubt, to trust in times of despair, to rejoice in times of blessing. And now we are asked to give in a time of need. Help us to meet this challenge. In Jesus' name.   Amen.

The following prayer, though not springing from the singing of a hymn, contains a similar theme.

O God, we know that only through devotion is any great thing done. Our offering of money is but one expression of our commitment to what you are doing through our church. Accept our gift, we pray. Amen.

The offertory is a very concrete way of showing our love of God, our sensitivity to the needs of others, and our concern for the work of the church. This prayer was written around that idea.

God, we make covenants with one another and with you. We know that these covenants are more than word agreements or silent understandings: They also involve concrete expression. The giving of our money—no easy thing—teaches us that. Amen.

Often when I place my offering in the plate as it is passed to me by a member of my church, I think of the many causes to which my gift goes. It is good to acknowledge this in the offertory prayer.

O Thou who hast in love given, who hast in beauty spoken, accept the gifts we bring. May they be used to spread the good word that the beauty of nature cannot compare with the beauty of the human spirit, made in your image. In Christ's name. Amen.

As with the offertory sentence, so with the prayer—the theme of joy is natural and instructive. Here are two prayers that include the joy theme. In one the joy is asked for; in the other it is self-evident.

O God of gifts, bless these gifts, and grant us joy for having given.

● ● ●

Dear God, we lay this offering before Thee both out of the obligation of stewardship and from the joy of being your children. Accept what we bring, in the name of the Model Steward, the blessed Son, our Lord. Amen.

Writing Offertory Prayers and Sentences

Preparation of the offertory prayers or sentences does not require the same energy and time as the preparation of the pastoral prayers, calls to worship, and readings. This does not mean they should be done without forethought; for if they are, they will most likely ramble. Also, if the pastor is giving the offertory prayer and he or she is unprepared, the prayer may include parts of the sermon, for that is what is uppermost in the preacher's mind by this point in the worship service.

The prayer or sentence may focus on the gift, the giver, and/or the giving. When the *gift* is uppermost, then the significance of it, the need for it, and the causes to which it will go may form the prayer. When the *giver* is uppermost, then the act of commitment and the joy in the heart of the giver are acknowledged. The person who is praying may ask God to bless the giver. It can be said that some give out of wealth, some out of poverty. When *giving* is uppermost, the joy of giving should be emphasized. Also, giving can be compared to receiving. The motives for giving can be referred to. And the larger meaning of giving, that is, the wider stewardship, is an appropriate element for a prayer or sentence which focuses on giving itself.

Once used, these prayers and sentences can, and ought to be, used over and over. Repetition has a way of dramatizing the significance of this part of the worship service. I often had worshipers come by and say how much a certain offertory sentence, which I used many times, meant to their worship experience.

Let me add one more word about the placement of the offertory prayer or sentence. It may be given either before or after the ushers collect the offering. It doesn't matter. If the prayer or word is given before the collection, the ushers ought to be in place at the front or back of the sanctuary. If it is after the offering, the ushers will bring the offering to the front for the dedication.

Chapter 5

Responsive Readings
and Litanies

The regular use of responsive readings indicates that the congregation is involved in worship at significant levels. The liturgical worship books have a reading for every occasion. Even the nonliturgical hymnals include readings. However, as with a tailored suit, there is nothing quite so meaningful as a reading prepared especially for an occasion in the worship life of your congregation.

There are other names for the readings. Sometimes they are called litanies. Literally, a litany is a prayer, but the word is used frequently to refer to a responsive reading. The reading may have a special title, such as "Covenant on Discipleship," or "Reading on Citizenship," or "Special Commissioning Ceremony." Regardless of the label, we are talking about a reading in which the congregation and others read responsively.

I believe the most meaningful readings allow the congregation to read substantive dialogue rather than merely respond with a repetitive phrase after the minister reads a long paragraph. In some litanies the congregation says nothing except something like, "God be praised." This phrase, or one of similar form, is repeated throughout the reading. Somehow, this practice does not seem to excite the intelligent person.

A Scripture-Based Reading

The Bible has many worship materials in it. These materials are especially evident in the Psalms. For example, Psalm 136 is a twenty-six-verse recital of praise, each verse ending with the phrase, "for his mercy endureth for ever." One can readily see how this psalm can be utilized as a responsive reading.

Psalm 150 may be made into a reading by the following pattern.

Minister: Praise ye the Lord. Praise God in his
              sanctuary:
Congregation: Praise him in the firmament of his
              power.
Minister: Praise him for his mighty acts:
Congregation: Praise him according to his excellent
              greatness.
Minister: Praise him with trumpet:
Congregation: Praise him with psaltery and harp.
Minister: Praise him with the timbrel and dance:
Congregation: Praise him with the stringed instruments
              and organs.
Minister: Praise him upon the loud cymbals:
Congregation: Praise him upon the high sounding
              cymbals.
Minister: Let every thing that hath breath praise
              the Lord.
Congregation: Praise ye the Lord.

Not all Scripture is ready-made for this kind of reading. There are some materials which, while clearly worship material, have to be adapted for the worship service. For example, the faith recital in Hebrews is probably too long for most worship services. For a chapel service at a seminary I adapted the faith recital (from the RSV) in the following style.

Minister: Now faith is the assurance of things hoped for,
              the conviction of things not seen.
Congregation: For by it the men of old received divine
              approval.
Minister: By faith we understand that the world was
              created by the word of God,
Congregation: So that what is seen was made out of things
              which do not appear.
Minister: By faith Abel offered to God a more acceptable
              sacrifice than Cain.
Congregation: By faith Enoch was taken up so that he should
              not see death.
Minister: By faith Noah . . . took heed and constructed
              an ark for the saving of his household.
Congregation: By faith Abraham obeyed when he was called to

go out to a place which he was to receive as an inheritance.

Minister: By faith Sarah herself received power to conceive . . . since she considered him faithful who had promised.

Congregation: By faith Moses . . . refused to be called the son of Pharaoh's daughter.

Minister: By faith the people crossed the Red Sea as if on dry land.

Congregation: By faith the walls of Jericho fell down.

Minister: By faith Rahab the harlot did not perish with those who were disobedient.

Congregation: And what more shall I say? For time would fail me to tell of Gideon, Barak, Samson, Jephthah, of David and Samuel and the prophets—

Minister: Who through faith conquered kingdoms, enforced justice, received promises,

Congregation: Stopped the mouths of lions, quenched raging fire, . . . won strength out of weakness.

Minister: Others suffered mocking and scourging, and even chains and imprisonment.

Congregation: They were stoned, they were sawn in two, they were killed with the sword.

Minister: Of whom the world was not worthy.

Then I went to other parts of the New Testament.

Minister: By faith Mary said to Gabriel, "Behold, I am the handmaid of the Lord; let it be to me according to your word."

Congregation: By faith Joseph took Mary to be his wife but knew her not until she had borne a son.

Minister: By faith Peter and Andrew left their nets and followed Jesus.

Congregation: By faith Stephen prayed, "Lord, do not hold this sin against them."

Minister: By faith Paul told the Athenians, "What therefore you worship as unknown, this I proclaim to you."

Congregation: Therefore, since we are surrounded by so great a cloud of witnesses,

Minister: Let us also lay aside every weight, and sin which clings so closely,

Congregation: And let us run with perseverance the race that is set before us,

Minister: Looking to Jesus the pioneer and perfecter of our faith,

Congregation: Who for the joy that was set before him endured the cross, despising the shame,

Minister: And is seated at the right hand of the throne of God.

Here is another example of the Scripture-based reading, taken from a chapel service on hope, based on Romans 8:18-25 (from RSV).

The Reality of Hope

Leader: I consider that the sufferings of this present time are not worth comparing with the glory that is to be revealed to us.

Congregation: For the creation waits with eager longing for the revealing of the sons of God;

Leader: For the creation was subjected to futility, not of its own will but by the will of him who subjected it in hope;

Congregation: Because the creation itself will be set free from its bondage to decay and obtain the glorious liberty of the children of God.

Leader: We know that the whole creation has been groaning in travail together until now;

Congregation: And not only the creation, but we ourselves, who have the first fruits of the Spirit, groan inwardly as we wait for adoption as sons, the redemption of our bodies.

Leader: For in this hope we were saved.

Congregation: Now hope that is seen is not hope.

Leader: For who hopes for what he sees?

Congregation: But if we hope for what we do not see, we wait for it with patience.

Historical Reading

Sometimes a reading can be formulated from historical excerpts. Here is an example of such a reading, taken from a chapel service on faith.

Minister: By faithing it Peter Waldo preached that the

Scriptures, rather than the pope, should be obeyed.

Congregation: By faithing it Francis of Assisi found a fraternity in all reality.

Minister: By faithing it Luther said at Worms, "I cannot and will not recant."

Congregation: By faithing it Helwys declared that people should "keep their consciences to God."

Minister: By faithing it Henry Dunster resigned at Harvard because he could not be silent about believer's baptism.

Congregation: By faithing it the founders of Southern Seminary refused to let the seminary die, rather pledging their own lives first.

Minister: By faithing it Pope John let some fresh air into the Catholic church.

Congregation: By faithing it Rabbi Heschel resisted the Vietnam war.

Minister: By faithing it Martin Luther King's eyes saw the glory and he inspired a people that they could overcome.

Congregation: And what more can we say? Time fails us to tell of all who in faith saw beyond hard times and believed the promise, even some among us here.

Litany of Commission/Ordination

The responsive reading is an engaging way of involving the entire congregation in services where ministers or deacons are being commissioned for their work. At the request of my pastor, Lee Stephens of the Englewood Baptist Church, I prepared the following readings for the commissioning of members of church committees and the ordination of deacons.

Litany of Commission

Minister: What can we affirm about this fellowship known as the Englewood Baptist Church?

All: That we are the people of God.

Minister: What is it that binds our fellowship?

All: In Jesus Christ is our unity.

Minister: To what purposes is this unity directed?

All: We exist to worship God, to learn, live, and share the faith, and to serve the world.

Minister: That's right, and today we confirm our fellow members who will lead us.

Congregation: Who among us has agreed to this work of God?

Chairpersons: We and our committee colleagues.

Congregation: Have you accepted this work willingly?

Chairpersons: Yes, we joyfully take on our responsibilities.

Congregation: Do you know how much depends on your loyalty?

Chairpersons: Yes, we understand the seriousness of our assignments.

Congregation: We then commission you in the name of the Christ.

Minister: And do you wish to ask anything of the congregation?

Chairpersons: We cannot fulfill our task without your prayers.

Congregation: Our prayers will be with you.

Minister: These duties we assume and these pledges we make are of God.

All: Then he surely will be with us.

Minister: So he will; so he will.

All: Then let us worship, learn, live, share, and serve.

Minister: Amen! Amen!

The Ordaining Covenant

Minister: You have heard the affirmations of faith of the persons chosen and confirmed by you to be your deacons. What is your pleasure concerning these brothers and sisters?

Congregation: We give praise for their faith and commitment, and we wish to ordain them.

Minister: What challenge concerning the faith have you for the ordinands?

Congregation: We charge them to be faithful to Jesus Christ, the Lord, and to teach and exemplify his truth.

Minister: What challenge concerning the church?

Congregation: We charge them to help keep unity in the church and to work to build up the church in its worship, learning, attendance, and financial support.

Minister: What challenge concerning the world?

Congregation: We charge them to lead us into the world as servants, meeting the needs of contemporary urban persons; and as witnesses, sharing the gospel with a lost world.

Minister: And you who are being ordained, what is your response to such a challenge?

Deacons: We are awed by such responsibilities and will need God's help and yours.

Minister: The Christ has already promised to be with us always.

Congregation: And we promise to support you, even as we have called you out from among us.

Deacons: Then we will work as best we can to demonstrate faith, build up the church, and lead the congregation into the world.

Minister: Are you ready to be ordained by this congregation with prayer and the touch?

Deacons: We are ready!

Minister: Let us now, by prayer and the laying on of hands, ordain these good servants to the deaconate of the Englewood Baptist Church.

Covenant on Citizenship

During any year there are special days on which readings add much to the worship experience, days such as Easter, July 4, Reformation Sunday, and Thanksgiving Sunday. Here is a reading which I created for Freedom '76 in San Antonio, Texas. The reading also has been used in some churches. Note the use of several groups of readers.

Covenant on Citizenship[1]

Leader: Where is our citizenship?

Group 1:   We are citizens of the state and members of the kingdom of God.

Group 2:   Let every person be subject to the governing authorities.

Group 3:   We must obey God rather than men.

Leader: And how is this dual citizenship to be expressed?

Group 1:   We are free to be patriotic.

Group 2:   We are free to be prophetic.

Group 3:   We are free to agree, free to dissent.

Leader: Free to be patriotic:

Group 1:   "Breathes there the man, with soul so dead,
Who never to himself hath said,
This is my own, my native land!"

Group 2: "'Tis the star-spangled banner;
Oh, long may it wave
O'er the land of the free,
And the home of the brave."

Group 3: "I love thy rocks and rills,
Thy woods and templed hills."

Leader: Free to be prophetic:

Group 1: "Confirm thy soul in self-control,
Thy liberty in law!"

Group 2: "That whenever any Form of Government becomes
destructive to these ends, it is the Right of the People
to alter or to abolish it."

Group 3: "Judge of the Nations,
spare us yet,
Lest we forget—lest we forget!"

Leader: Free to agree:

Group 1: I will preserve, protect, and defend the Constitution
of the United States.

Group 2: "Who more than self their country loved,
And mercy more than life!"

Group 3: "O Motherland,
we pledge to thee,
Head, heart, and hand
through the years to be!"

Leader: Free to dissent:

Group 1: "Congress shall make no law . . . abridging the
freedom of speech, or . . . to petition the Government for a redress of grievances."

Group 2: "Give me liberty or give me death!"

Group 3: "I . . . have a dream . . . that . . . brotherhood will
be more than a few words at the end of a prayer, but
rather the first order of business on every legislative
agenda."

Leader: What, then, can we promise our country and the
kingdom of God?

Group 1: To listen intently.

Group 2: To think clearly.

Group 3: To act wisely.

Leader: We promise to listen intently

Group 1: To our leaders who are charged with the common
good,

Group 2: To those who see the issues differently,

Group 3: To the majority and the minority.
Leader: We promise to think clearly
Group 1: To affirm the past but not to be bound by it,
Group 2: To explore all sides of every question,
Group 3: To try to overcome personal bias.
Leader: We promise to act wisely
Group 1: To do what seems best as we understand the options,
Group 2: To do thoroughly what we begin,
Group 3: To seek God's will in everything we do.
Leader: We are citizens of the kingdom and the state.
Group 1: We are free for patriotism,
          free for reform.
Group 2: We are free to agree,
          free to dissent.
Group 3: We promise to listen,
          think, and act as
          persons free in Jesus Christ.
All: "Grant us wisdom, grant us courage,
          That we fail not man nor thee"!

Covenant on Discipleship

The writing of readings does not have to wait for special seasons and events. A sermon on love, joy, stewardship, or any other topic can spawn a litany. The following reading[2] was made for Freedom '76, but it can be utilized in the congregation.

Leader: You are now invited into a time
          of collecting your thoughts and feelings
          as an artist does before a concert appearance,
Group 1: As an athlete before an Olympic contest,
Group 2: As a student before an examination,
Group 3: As a speaker before a major address,
All: As Jesus Christ in Gethsemane.
Leader: Who are we in this moment of remembering?
Group 1: We are members of the family of man;
Group 2: We are children of God;
Group 3: We are disciples of Jesus the Christ.
All: "You are a chosen race,
          a royal priesthood, . . .
          God's own people."
Leader: How did we come to be who we are?
Group 1: We were born into the world family;

Group 2: God the Father made us his children;
Group 3: We chose for ourselves to
          be disciples of the Christ.
All: "It is he that hath made us . . .
          we are his people."
Leader: What will be the fruit of this being?
Group 1: We will relate to all as brother/sister;
Group 2: We will show what God is like;
Group 3: We will follow the work of Jesus.
All: "Blessed are your eyes, for they see:
          and your ears, for they hear."
Leader: How will we relate to all as brother/sister?
Group 1: By feeding the hungry,
Group 2: By comforting the distressed,
Group 3: By honoring the personal dignity of all persons.
All: "When you did it to my brothers,
          you did it to me."
Leader: How will we show what God is like?
Group 1: By working for peace wherever there is war,
Group 2: By working for the civil liberties of all,
Group 3: By working toward a healthy use of environment and
          energy.
All: "Let us make man . . . and let them
          have dominion . . . over all the earth."
Leader: How will we follow the work of Jesus?
Group 1: By finding his will in making career choices,
Group 2: By considering his life in making ethical decisions,
Group 3: By seeking his spirit in family relationships.
All: "Birds . . . have nests;
          but the Son of man has nowhere to lay his head."
Leader: And what else will we do?
Group 1: We will show that freedom in Christ
          is neither uncontrolled permissiveness
          nor dehumanizing slavery;
Group 2: We will adopt life-styles that show
          the radical claim of the gospel
          upon our lives;
Group 3: We will keep hope alive in the
          midst of the most desperate situations.
Leader: "Go and make disciples, and remember,
          I am with you."
All: "For not with swords loud clashing,

Nor roll of stirring drums;
With deeds of love and mercy,
The heavenly kingdom comes."

A Prayer at Fasting's End

I was once asked to prepare a prayer-reading that would conclude a time of fasting and introduce the bringing of contributions for the hungry. This same kind of reading can be used for the service on Pledge Sunday, or as a commitment for other occasions.

A Prayer at Fasting's End

Leader: O God, Maker of heaven and of the earth:
Group 1: O God of all time, and of every age:
Group 2: O God of all persons, and of every individual:
Group 3: O God, everywhere and here:
All: We pray to you; we pray to you.
Leader: O listening God, hear our confessions:
Group 1: We have not fully affirmed that this is the place we ought to be.
Group 2: We have not fully lived this moment as significant to all of our days.
Group 3: We have not fully celebrated being with our brothers and sisters.
All: Forgive us. Forgive us. Forgive us.
Leader: O speaking God, talk to us.
Group 1: Tell us how to find a place to stand in this unstable world.
Group 2: Tell us how to give meaning to each moment that we are alive.
Group 3: Tell us how to meet one another as "Thou" rather than "It."
All: Speak to us. Speak to us. Speak to us.
Leader: O accepting God, receive our gifts of love.
Group 1: We offer our minds, dedicated to your work in the world.
Group 2: We offer our strength, ready to be harnessed for your service.
Group 3: We offer our hearts and souls, ready to understand and feel and be all you have intended.
All: Accept our offering. Accept our offering.
Leader: O acting God, work your will through our willing lives.

Group 1: Today we have not eaten so that our brothers and sisters might have bread.

Group 2: We have identified with the hungry, for we have wanted food but have not eaten.

Group 3: And we lay at the altar the fruit of this day of fasting.

All: Accept our work as an expression of your work upon the earth. In the name of the Christ—who knew a time and place, and who saw people as persons, and who did your will—receive what we now bring. Amen.

Leader: Amen. Amen. But tomorrow, will not you have bread and more than enough, while others will continue in their hunger?

All: Yes, but in this day of fasting we have felt the plight of the nations and have seen the despair of the earth's people. And the Christ has been born anew in us. Thus will we continue, as he told us, to feed the hungry, for in that very act we will be meeting God.

Leader: And do you know what price this commitment might exact?

All: Yes. It will mean rethinking our entire life-style, lowering our standard of living, and participating more in decisions made at all levels of government.

Leader: So be it.

All: So be it.

Leader: God help us.

All: God help us.

Leader: Amen.

All: Amen.

A Call to Worship Reading

A responsive reading may also be used as a call to worship. In this case, it should be brief and follow the rules for good calls to worship. Here is an example of this kind of call.

Minister: Good morning.

Congregation: Good morning, in the name of the Christ.

Minister: How is it that we meet in his name?

Congregation: We are redeemed through his life.

Minister: How is it that we needed to be saved?

Congregation: We sinned against our Maker.

Minister: What was that sin?

Congregation: We misused our freedom as children of God.

Minister: And what was sin's consequence?
Congregation: We were alienated from God.
Minister: What shall we say of our salvation?
Congregation: Praise the Father; praise the Son.

Non-Responsive Readings

Not all readings have to be responsive. For example, the reading of Scripture by one person is a regular feature of most worship services. This element in worship may be called Bible Reading, Scripture Reading, New Testament Lesson, Old Testament Lesson. However, other resources may be utilized for such readings. One minister of music I worked with often had newspaper stories read. One such reading on a local problem led to intense congregational interest, the organization of a special study, and finally the formation of a mission action group to do something about the problem. Another worship leader read from biographies of great persons. I have had persons read excerpts from helpful books and major writers and from good sermons. Once, for a chapel service on hope a reader read Erik Erikson's beautiful account of the relationship between the care of the infant and the development of hope. Sometimes pastors have sermons which are especially remembered and popular. Excerpts from these can be very effective as readings for worship. I think you can see the limitless possibilities for this kind of reading.

How to Write a Reading

We have seen that readings can be found in Scripture, other literature, history, biography, and sermons. They may be created for special seasons, days, or events, such as Race Relations Sunday, Pledge Sunday, Independence Day, Easter Day, Thanksgiving Sunday, etc. They may involve one reader, two readers, or in some cases several groups of respondents to the minister's lines.

As with the calls to worship and prayers, I now want us to create a reading. But before getting our creative energies flowing on some subject, let us look at some qualifications for readings. First, the congregation ought to have more to do than read the same phrase over and over after the minister reads the good stuff. Second, the lines for both the leader and the congregation ought to be brief. Long lines are difficult to read, and often the focus of the reading is lost. Third, the reading does not have to be poetic. It should avoid unnecessary wordiness, but it doesn't have to be as tight as what a poet would write, and certainly it need not rhyme.

Let us suppose that we have a worship service coming soon, a service in which we are to have a dedication of a newborn child. It is the kind of event suited to a reading; so let us write one.

First, let us write down some ideas, phrases, or words that come to mind as we think about the service.

> child of God . . . innocence . . . potential . . . spiritual guidance . . . nurture . . . education . . . growth . . . image of God . . . responsibility . . . hopes and dreams . . . God our Father . . . new creation . . . patterns of development . . . stages of growth . . . crawl, walk, run . . . what children grow up to be . . . the child belongs to all of us in the church . . . Jesus' presentation at the temple

That activity, for me, took about five minutes. Our next task is to consider the persons and groups who will be participating in the service. At least three groups or persons come to mind: the minister, the parents, and the congregation. Of course, the child is there but has nothing to say or do.

Now for the writing:

Dedication Litany

Minister: We are here today to present __(child's name)__ to the church and to dedicate her to God. Who brings the child for this holy purpose?

Parents: We, her parents, bring __(first name)__ to be dedicated to God.

Minister: What can we affirm about __(first name)__?

Congregation: That she is made in the image of God, and is a child of God by creation.

Minister: What will the child be told about her history?

Congregation: We will tell her about Abraham, the father of our faith; about Moses who led our ancestors out of bondage; about the Jewish hope for a Messiah; about Jesus Christ the Savior; and about the history of the church as the new people of God.

Minister: Who is responsible to help the child know God as her Father, to know her history, to grow up in the faith, and personally decide her relationship to Jesus Christ?

Parents: We are the persons primarily responsible for this awesome work.

Minister: Is anyone else to help with the child's spiritual
                   guidance?
Congregation: Yes, we, too, will share in _(first name)'s_ growth,
                   for she belongs to us as well.
Minister: Then, may God be with us.
Congregation: God help us. Amen.
Minister: Amen.

This writing took me about thirty-five minutes. The entire
activity was done in forty-five minutes. Usually, more time will be
required for creating a special litany. Of course, after experience in
such writing, the task becomes easier. Besides the rewards of creating
something, you also feel the satisfaction that everyone in the
congregation will get to participate in the dedication. This means,
then, that the whole people of God are dedicating the child and that it
is not being done only by an ordained minister. Since we just created
this child dedication litany, I am only supposing that such a reward
would be the result, but that supposition is based on remembering
what I felt when my congregation used my readings for commissioning committee chairpersons and ordaining deacons. I remember
thinking, "All of us are setting these persons to these important
tasks."

Chapter 6

Christmas, Easter, and Pentecost

All of us have favorite people, things, and seasons. You and I attach ourselves to a special person, a special thing, a special time. My preferred religious season is Advent. Every year in my church a child walks uncharacteristically seriously down the aisle of the sanctuary, with flaming candle in hand, to light the first Advent candle. Someday the child will understand what we older persons know, namely, that in this moment we are lighting a candle against the darkness, to say that what God did in Bethlehem he is getting ready to do all over again and that we must make preparation if we are to see this thing which is to come to pass.

The child's father's generation of Baptists gave no recognition to Advent, for it was seen as the property of the liturgical churches with little meaning in the free church tradition. However, the celebration of Advent and other festivals and holy days is being returned to its rightful place in Christian worship. In our time, some 450 years after the Reformation, perspectives are somewhat more balanced and reactionary extremes more lovingly modified.

The three most holy and joyful days are Christmas, Easter, and Pentecost. On these days we remember the birth of Jesus, the Christ, and his resurrection and the recognition of the Holy Spirit in power. The Christmas and Easter festivals have seasons of preparation: Advent for Christmas, Lent and Holy Week for Easter. Without this preparation these holy days come on us and go, and we miss the drama, the meaning, and the blessing which they offer to the spiritually prepared. For example, by the time Christmas Day arrives, the rush of the social calendar and the anguish of the commercial dimension have squelched any real spiritual feeling for what is about to happen. A single Christmas sermon on the evils of materialism and selfishness usually comes too late to redeem the season. It produces much guilt but little positive religious experience or change. The celebration of Advent will give our people an alternative to the holiday fury that begins after Thanksgiving and lasts until the stores close on Christmas Eve.

Advent for me is a time of renewing the wellsprings of hope, a time of expectancy that the Christ who came still comes; Advent says that just as he came in Bethlehem so many years ago, so he is getting ready to come where I live. Thus, I worship and wait as we light the candles of Advent, for I know that on Christmas Sunday (the Sunday following Christmas if the holiday falls on any day other than Sunday) when we light the Christmas candle, we shall dance and sing, bringing out our songs of greatest joy and our prayers of highest praise. Christ, the Savior, is born! The Advent prepares me for the grand day.

But there is more. Preparation is not the only reason for celebrating holy seasons. Such a celebration provides an opportunity to identify with the broad sweep of Christian history. Roots of Advent are found in the fourth century; Lent is from the apostolic times; and Holy Week was practiced in some form by the third century. Such history ought not to be so easily abandoned, unless, of course, that history has hopelessly lost its meaning—as when Martin Luther was so convinced of the corruption of worship that after his confrontation with the Catholic church, he ignored much of the traditional Holy Week celebration, although he kept the sermons of Holy Thursday and Good Friday.

It seems to me that Pentecost especially illustrates the point of identification with a long history. Like the birth and resurrection narratives which combine materials to form a whole, so the Acts 2 passage contains witnesses to an intense experience in the life of the early church. As we read these gripping accounts of a very significant event, we feel as if we are there hearing the wind, seeing fire, hearing the witnesses, sharing the fellowship. In Pentecost worship, we are indeed in touch with Christian experience and church celebration which are from the earliest of our history.

Still another reason for recognizing a holy season is that it is a way of identifying with contemporary Christianity all over the world. For all that sets us off as Baptists, Episcopalians, Nazarenes, Catholics et al., we do have much in common. Holy Week is the grand example of this commonality. The Christ who was killed, buried, and resurrected is the same for all of us. To be sure, we have our differing approaches to the full meaning of the atonement and resurrection, but for all of us Easter is the central event which gives the church existence and sustenance.

When Christians around the world are gathering for Holy Thursday Communion or to hear Good Friday sermons on Jesus' words from the cross, we ought to want to be in on it. Even with the time zone differentials, there still is a simultaneity about these celebrations that adds depth and breadth to their meaning and gives us a feeling of communion with Christians everywhere.

The opportunity to witness is another reason for celebrating these seasons. In Advent we show the world what we see in the Christmas event. The commercial sector clearly demonstrates its view of Christmas. To be sure, it mixes a little religion with its message by using favorite carols, but that hardly gets at the radicality of the gospel message with which Bethlehem is concerned. That is our job, and waiting until Christmas will not accomplish it. The same is true for Holy Week. Our participation in reenacting the dramatic events of this, the darkest and brightest of weeks, is a witness to the world of the mission of Jesus.

These celebrations are not the time to play with liturgical toys, thus demeaning their significance. The color and drama are not ends in themselves but are witnesses to the basic events in our faith. This is why you will want to celebrate these special times in ways compatible with the style of your congregation. It probably would be a mistake to enter fully into these seasons all at once. The advice I would give is to start with what you have and build from that. For example, if you already have Christmas, Palm Sunday, and Easter, expand your Christmas preaching to two or three sermons, and add the Lord's Supper on Holy Thursday. The next step might be to add the lighting of candles on the four Sundays of Advent, Good Friday services, and the recognition of Pentecost Sunday. From this point you might move into Lent and then add the other elements—full services, banners, Chrismon tree, etc. In a few years you will have led your congregation into full-scale celebrations of these pivotal seasons of faith and worship.

Advent and Christmas

Let us now examine how the Advent and Christmas drama is done. The Sundays of Advent are the four before Christmas. The Sunday after Christmas is Christmas Sunday. When Christmas comes on Sunday, then it is, of course, Christmas Sunday, and the four prior Sundays comprise the Advent.

A candle is lit on each Sunday until all four are alight on the fourth Sunday of Advent. Then the Christmas candle may be lit on Christmas Eve or at special services on Christmas Day.

The Christmas candle is white, the traditional color for holy days. The candles for Advent Sundays vary in color. Some churches use four violet or blue candles. Either color symbolizes penitence, a religious experience in preparation for a great event. Some churches light three purple candles as a sign of royalty and a pink candle for the Rose of Sharon. Green, a popular Christmas color, may be used, but it has no liturgical significance for the Advent season.

Each congregation, in the free church tradition may show any color or color combination as long as it is appropriate to what is being symbolized. The five candles may be in candlesticks or placed in or around a wreath. The Advent wreath, introduced by German Protestants, symbolizes life. It may rest on the Communion table along with the candles or hang in a special place.

The Sunday services are more intense if the lighting of the candles is done during the service. On the first Sunday all the candles are "dark"; then at some point the first candle is lit. On the second Sunday that candle is burning as the service begins, and then the second candle is lit during the service. This sequence continues until all Advent candles are aglow as you enter on Christmas Sunday; then on that day the Christmas candle is lit during the service, even though it may also have been burning for Christmas Eve services.

There are different ways of handling the lighting of the candles. You can have representatives of the age groups in your church take turns. Or children only may be asked to light the candles. A family of five may be used. Regardless of who does the lighting, it is an inspiring moment in the worship service; and as the number of glowing candles increases, so do the drama and the meaning.

Aids to the Celebration

Banners may also be created for use during Advent and Christmas. They enrich the physical setting in which the season is celebrated. The banners can bear religious symbols or words or a combination. For example, a banner might carry a star and the words, "Christ is born." Some appropriate symbols are the Bethlehem star, the shepherd's staff, the lamb, the rose, the Chi-Rho, the anchor cross, and the dove. In my church in Kansas City the banners followed the sermon subjects and were brought into the sanctuary as part of the procession. Each was put in a special place the Sunday it represented the theme; after that it was placed with the others around the sanctuary.

Paintings and sculptures can be displayed in the vestibule or on the Communion table. Prints of famous art may be available at your public library or in the homes of some of your members. Among the more popular works are Botticelli's *The Nativity,* Piero della Francesca's *The Nativity,* and Giotto's *Virgin and Child.* If you are emphasizing the ministry of Christ, use Rembrandt's *Christ with the Sick Around Him.*

Another form of celebrating the season is the use of a Chrismon tree. A Chrismon, literally, is a Christ monogram, a symbol representing Jesus Christ. The term, however, broadly includes religious symbols of all sorts—crosses, lambs, wheat and grapes, Bibles, the Greek letters alpha and omega, Trinity triangles, eternity circles, etc. The symbols are made by church members and are placed on the Chrismon tree in the sanctuary. The tree can be trimmed on any Sunday in Advent. The tree has a long tradition of symbolizing life. But instead of people exchanging gifts under it or waiting for Santa Claus to appear, the religious is emphasized in the Chrismon tree.

A lay person in the Crescent Hill Church in Louisville introduced our church to the Chrismon concept. She and others of us sponsored workshops for making Chrismons and understanding the symbols. This activity added even more depth to an already rich Advent experience. Chrismons may be cut from Styrofoam and decorated with ribbon, sequins, and jewelry. Or they may be made of other substances and painted.

Introducing Advent to Your Church

The introduction of Advent into your Christmas worship may be done gradually. Chances are that you already have a traditional musical program. You can add a Christmas Eve service and preach two or more "Christmas" sermons rather than only one, without much ado about the word "Advent." Once you feel comfortable that the sermon pattern is taking hold and giving meaning to the season, you can introduce the wreath and candles; then, in time, you can add the banners and the Chrismon tree.

Since the wreath and candles may be the most foreign to many worshipers, both of them may be suggested for use in the home before they are introduced into the services at church. The same motif is followed here as at church and includes the wreath, candles, Scripture reading, prayer, and singing. This home service can be on Saturdays or Sundays. It is important that all members of the family participate in the services.

Christmas Preaching

Besides the symbolism and activities, the unfolding Advent drama needs good preaching. You have the great Isaiah passages of promise and the birth of Christ narratives. There are the penitential and celebrative psalms and the whole range of New Testament accounts of the works of Jesus. What is he like, this coming One? What does he do? What does he show and demand?

Elwyn Hays, former pastor at my Englewood church, preached on five topics—"The Lord's Servant," "The Unsung," "Waiting for a Message," "Recognizing the Light," and "They Called Him Jesus." Another pastor followed this pattern: "The Hope of Advent," "The Peace of Advent," "The Love of Advent," "The Joy of Advent," and "The Faith of Christmas."

The preaching can include missionary, social, and eschatological emphases. For example, Southern Baptists emphasize foreign missions in early December. This can be made a part of the Advent. The social fabric of the preaching of the gospel is without dispute, and its inclusion in Advent sermons could provide a needed corrective to the lavish attention we pour out on our family and friends amidst widespread poverty. And, finally, to talk of the birth of Jesus is also to look to his Second Coming. Bishop Robinson combines the social and eschatalogical by the use of the parable of the last judgment. His sermon is that when the King judges us in the end, it will be on the basis of how we saw his coming in the everyday needs of persons around us, thus giving attention to that aspect of the Advent drama which presents the Christ as the One who comes even now. This thought gave birth to a responsive benediction which has been used in the chapel of the Seminary where I teach and in my church: The Christ has come; and still comes.

Here are some examples of Advent and Christmas services.

Christmas Eve Service of Nine Lessons and Carols

Hymn "O Come, All Ye Faithful" (Stanza 1)
Invocation
The First Lesson   *An Ancient Vision,* Isaiah 11:1-10
"Lo, How a Rose E'er Blooming"
The Second Lesson   *A Promised Sign,* Isaiah 7:10-14
"He Shall Feed His Flock"
The Third Lesson   *A Continuing Hope,* Micah
   5:1-7
"O Come, O Come, Emmanuel"
Instrumental Interlude on "Silent Night"

Lighting of the Christmas Candle
The Fourth Lesson   *A Reassuring Dream,* Matthew
   1:18-25
"What Child Is This"
The Fifth Lesson *A Fateful Journey,* Luke 2:1-5
"O Little Town of Bethlehem"
The Sixth Lesson   *A Joyful Expectation,* Luke 2:8-14
"Angels We Have Heard on High"
Instrumental Interlude on "Let All Mortal Flesh
   Keep Silence"
The Seventh Lesson   *A Holy Birth,* Luke 2:6-7
"Joy to the World" or "O Come, Little Children"
The Eighth Lesson   *A Visit from Sages,* Matthew 2:1-2, 11
"Hark! the Herald Angels Sing" or "We Three Kings"
The Ninth Lesson   *A Later Editorial,* John 1:1-14
"Fairest Lord Jesus"
Benedictory Prayer
Benedictory Reading
   Minister: The Christ Has Come;
   Congregation: And Still Comes.
"O Come, All Ye Faithful" (Stanzas 2 and 3) or "Joy to the
   World"

An alternate title is "A Service of Scripture and Music." Or the
word "reading" may be substituted for "lesson." This service has a
form which could be used each year; thus, it would become a
tradition.

Advent in the Home

The First Sunday in Advent—
   Read Luke 1:26-33
      Mary learns that she will be Jesus' mother.
   Light the First Candle
   Sing "O Come, All Ye Faithful"
   Pray, "We thank you, God, for our family.
      We thank you for our church. We
      thank you for Jesus Christ. Help us
      this year, as we remember his life,
      to learn how to help others as he did. Amen."
The Second Sunday in Advent—
   Read Luke 2:1-5
      Mary and Joseph make a trip to Bethlehem.

Light the Second Candle
Sing "Silent Night"
Pray, "God, we thank you for Mary and Joseph
and for their care of Jesus when he was
growing up. Help our family members to love one another as Mary, Joseph, Jesus, and his
brothers and sisters loved one another. Amen."

The Third Sunday in Advent—
Read Luke 2:8-15
Something happy happens to some shepherds.
Light the Third Candle
Sing "O Little Town of Bethlehem"
Pray, "We are joyful, O God, as were the
shepherds, over what you have done in
sending Jesus Christ. Help us to show
this joy in our experiences during this
week. Amen."

The Fourth Sunday in Advent—
Read Luke 2:6-7
Jesus Christ is born in Bethlehem.
Light the Fourth Candle
Sing "Joy to the World"
Pray, "Dear God, we are thankful for these
brief times our family has had to-
gether, preparing for the meaning of
Christmas. Help us, above all else,
to remember that Christmas is the time
when you give us the good gift of
Jesus Christ. Amen."

Christmas Eve, Christmas Day, or Christmas Sunday
Read John 1:1-14
Who did people believe Jesus was?
Light the Christmas Candle
Sing "Fairest Lord Jesus"
Pray (Have spontaneous prayers by members
of the family)

The Sunday Advent Services

Obviously, the Sunday services will have to be altered in order to
include the Advent and Christmas suggestions. However, it probably
is not wise to depart too radically from the forms to which your
congregation is accustomed. The lighting of the candle will be new.

The procession of the choir and worship leaders adds a celebrative note. The reading of both Old and New Testament lessons gives the services a feel for the old and the new. And, of course, beyond these the content of the music and sermon let the worshipers know that the holy season of Christmas is here again.

Holy Week and Easter

Throughout the history of the church Easter has been the "Great Day." It has been preceded by Holy Week and Lent (actually, Holy Week is the last week of Lent) although some of these preparatory activities were ignored after the Protestant Reformation. As you can imagine, there has been, and still is, considerable variation in the way these activities have been and are managed. The pattern that seems most established in Protestant worship is Palm Sunday, Maundy Thursday, Good Friday, and Easter. However, some churches include the full season of Lent in their Easter preparation.

Lent

If you choose to celebrate Lent, there are appropriate ways to approach it in the free church tradition and still be faithful to its character as it has evolved in history. The two historic features of the season are fasting and the instruction of baptismal candidates. These practices can be translated into a time of deepening the spiritual life and of increasing our knowledge of basic Christian doctrine.

Let us examine the matter of repentance and fasting and then move to the incorporation of theological study during Lent. The repentance and fasting can be both individual and collective. It consists of the sharing of one's religious experience and may even eventuate in the making of public commitments by church members. Thus, this deepening of the spiritual life can be worked at individually and in groups and, if desired, affirmed before the entire worshiping congregation.

There are several kinds of small groups. The Lenten small groups should be formed for the purpose of sharing what is happening in our lives. Encounter and therapy groups are best reserved for other seasons. The sharing groups will need to meet weekly. The following elements can be included in the group meetings.

First, the reading of a Scripture and/or some piece of contemporary religious writing, such as an inspirational article from a magazine. This reading will be done in silence.

Second, the breaking of the silence: Name someone ahead

of time to do this. The designated breaker-of-the-silence simply says at the agreed-upon time, "I now break the silence."

Third, the sharing of experience: This sharing may come out of the reading or from events of the immediate week.

Fourth, the reporting of progress in deepening the spiritual life: If the group has covenanted to keep certain disciplines, such as daily Bible reading and/or helping someone outside the family, allow some time for the group members to share how they are progressing. This kind of honest sharing will establish strong bonds of love and build Christian character.

Fifth, praying together.

At the individual level of participation in Lent, fortunately the books abound on strengthening one's devotion. Two favorites among the classics are Augustine's *Confessions* and Pascal's *Pensees*. Another inspiring book is *Bonaventure: The Soul's Journey,* translated by Ewert Cousins, which was my Lenten reading one year. Besides the classics, there are the sermons of Fosdick, Niebuhr, and Tillich, to be borrowed from the minister's shelf. And, of course, every publishing house has a long list of devotional and inspirational books.

The public dedications can be encouraged in both regular and special services, such as revivals. This emphasis on commitment will not be a general call at the end of a worship service. Rather, the pastor will, in ways appropriate to each congregation, let it be known that the Lenten season will be a time for persons to reconsider their commitment to God, the church, and the world. The idea is that persons will feel free at any service to come to the altar and let their experiences be known.

In keeping with the dating of Lent, the emphasis on deepening the Christian experience should begin on Ash Wednesday with a special service and call to repentance and Christian growth. Ash Wednesday is dated forty days before Easter, not including Sundays.

This brings us to the other approach to Lent—the doctrinal studies. This can be done through preaching, regular church study classes, and special classes. The study can be built around a church's articles of faith or the traditional Apostles' Creed. Also, a more formal systematic study may be offered. Or the study may begin by having the participants write down what they believe about the classical doctrines. These writings, then, will become the basis for the discussions. We have often wondered why after so many sermons and church school lessons our people still don't know what they believe. Perhaps a part of the answer is that we have been busy telling them what to believe but have not asked what they believe and utilized the answers as a beginning point in helping these persons to build more adequate doctrinal understanding.

Worship services can be built around the major doctrines of the church. For example, beginning with the doctrine of creation, services can be devoted to different tenets, leading finally to the cross and resurrection. Besides the preaching on these doctrines, special readings and dramatic presentations may be a part of such services. The readings can appropriately be taken from whatever confession of faith to which your church subscribes. The selections may be read in unison or divided into antiphons.

Palm Sunday

Palm Sunday is the day for celebrating a special visit by Jesus to Jerusalem. This visit culminated in his death and included several key encounters and meetings with adversaries and friends. However, the entrance to the city elicited a spontaneous demonstration of popularity.

In contemporary practice we can take one of two approaches to worship on this day. One way of celebrating the day is by the joy motif. Under this approach the content of the service deals with significant events in the life of Jesus—with his thought and work. The alternative is to use Palm Sunday to put into perspective the events of Holy Week. This approach recognizes that in the backdrop of joy and praise looms the cross on which he was executed, and reminds the worshipers how quickly the plaudits of others can turn to the demand for severe punishment. In the Roman Catholic church this theme is present in the reading of the Passion narrative in Matthew.

The service will include readings from the life and teachings of Jesus. The selections will say, in effect, "Let us remember what Jesus did and said." A traditional Scripture for the day is Philippians 4:4-9. This material can be put in the form of a responsive reading.

A procession at the beginning of the service can be especially celebrative and set the tone for the service. The choir can come in singing an "Alleluia" or speaking it. Children, with their natural joy, might be enlisted to be included in this part of the service.

A more dramatic approach would be to have persons, dressed in first-century Palestinian clothes, reenact the entry of Jesus into the city. At the end of the service the light can be dimmed, with a spot focusing on a cross in the baptistry.

Preaching for Palm Sunday builds around events and teachings in the life of Jesus. This, of course, is a vast resource for sermons. Themes of integrity, courage, vocation, meaning, and joy are appropriate.

Holy Thursday

Holy Thursday has had many designations: Thursday of the Lord's Supper, birth of the chalice, birth of the Sacrament, and Maundy Thursday, a misuse of the Latin word *Mandatum,* which designates the washing of feet rite. The major element of the service is the Lord's Supper. The washing of feet has a place in the history of the day, and the service of darkness (Tenebrae) is celebrated by some churches on Thursday.

The Holy Thursday service will include the traditional accounts of and references to the Last Supper and betrayal as found in the New Testament. The manner of participating in the service will vary with different congregations. As I said in the Introduction, I will not deal with how to celebrate the Supper.

A church wishing to incorporate the washing of feet will, of course, be faced with practical problems more demanding than those of the Supper. In addition, our social inhibitions may prohibit participation by all worshipers. If this is the case, the worship leader and selected members of the church may reenact the footwashing before the congregation. There is no greater symbol of service, humility, and acceptance than this act. Jesus himself said, "If I then, your Lord . . . , have washed your feet; ye also ought to wash one another's feet" (John 13:14).

Drama can be effective for this service. The Supper or the betrayal and arrest can be acted out. In one such service a youth drama group pantomimed the Lord's Supper as the congregation celebrated the event.

Good Friday

Known by some as Black Friday, this day has always been a day of mourning and fasting. The primary mode of recognizing the day is the hours of darkness (noon to three o'clock) service in which the Lord's last words are read and interpreted. The service of darkness (Tenebrae) is sometimes included in the Good Friday schedule. The Lord's Supper also has had a place in the Friday celebrations, but it is best done on Holy Thursday.

The hours of darkness service is often an ecumenical one. Local ministers are invited to take the last words of Jesus and preach on them. Congregational singing and prayers also are included. The worshipers may come and go at any time during the three-hour service. This service is a grand opportunity for Christians of different beliefs to gather around a central event of the faith shared by all churches. Here are the words from the cross, traditionally a part of the hours of darkness service.

"Father, forgive them; for they know not what
they do."
(Luke 23:34)
"To day shalt thou be with me in paradise."
(Luke 23:43)
"Woman, behold thy son! Behold thy mother!"
(John 19:26-27)
"My God, my God, why hast thou forsaken me?"
(Matthew 27:46)
"I thirst."
(John 19:28)
"It is finished."
(John 19:30)
"Father, into thy hands I commend my spirit."
(Luke 23:46)

The Tenebrae service (not reserved solely for Friday) is a gift of the Roman Catholic church. Fifteen candles (in the form of a triangle) denoting Christ and the prophets who foretold his coming are extinguished one by one, until the upper one alone remains lit. This candle, still burning, is put under the altar. In some Protestant services there is no definite symbolism in the number of candles, and all candles are extinguished. Other symbolism for the candles might be for Christ and the apostles, for the Gospel writers, for the Sermon on the Mount, or for the last words of Jesus. The service is, as you would know, one of great solemnity.

The same Scriptures used for the hours of darkness can be used for the service of darkness. A special feature might be a requiem by the choir. The intent of this service is that the congregation feel the smothering shroud of darkness and suffering. The worship leader must resist introducing the Easter message into the service. That joyful part of the drama must wait until resurrection day.

Here is an example of the service of darkness. The music should include congregational singing, choral music, and solos, or duets, etc.

Service of Darkness
Matthew 5:1-12

Call to worship
Invocation

Lesson 1, Matthew 5:1-3
Music
Extinguish first candle

Lesson 2, Matthew 5:4
Music
Extinguish second candle

Lesson 3, Matthew 5:5
Music
Extinguish third candle

Lesson 4, Matthew 5:6
Music
Extinguish fourth candle

Lesson 5, Matthew 5:7
Music
Extinguish fifth candle

Lesson 6, Matthew 5:8
Music
Extinguish sixth candle

Lesson 7, Matthew 5:9
Music
Extinguish seventh candle

Lesson 8, Matthew 5:10
Extinguish eighth candle
Homily on Holy Week events up to the crucifixion
Prayer
Placing of ninth candle under the Communion
   table (altar)

Saturday

Services are generally not celebrated on Saturday. Jesus is in the tomb. However, the church sanctuary should be open on this day for Christians to come by to pray. The Bible on the Communion table could be open to the events of Holy Week. The single candle, not extinguished at the Tenebrae service, can be brought out. This is not the white candle representing the Easter light. One of the church's ministers or other leaders will be "on duty" at the back of the sanctuary to pass the peace to persons as they leave the sanctuary. The leader says, "May the peace of God be with you." And the worshiper responds, "And with you."

Easter Day

The resurrection day arrives. The violent events of the week and the darkness of Friday have passed. The gray sabbath is gone. It is Easter and the Christ is alive. The powers of death could not hold him. He is alive! Surely it is presumptuous for me to suggest what to do with worship on this day. Without even thinking, we know what the Easter sermon must be about.

Thus, my suggestions are given only as they connect this joyful day with the other events of the week. If you have had a Tenebrae service and left the sanctuary in darkness on Friday night, then you may want to have the lights off as the worshipers come in for the Easter worship. Then as the service begins and as the choir processes, the lights are turned on, the instruments sound in full, and all sing of Easter joy.

Some important sculptures, if you can find miniatures, are Michelangelo's *Pieta,* F. Rude's *Christ Crowned with Thorns,* and a wood carving, *Gethsemane,* by Ivan Mestrovic. There are many paintings dramatizing the events of Holy Week and Easter:

Salvador Dali, *The Sacrament of the Lord's
   Supper*
Phillipe de Champaigne, *The Last Supper*
Tintoretto, *The Last Supper*
El Greco, *The Agony in the Garden*
Rembrandt, *The Agony in the Garden*
Peter Brueghel, *Christ Carrying the Cross*
Rembrandt, *Christ Crucified Between Two
   Thieves*
Delacroix, *Christ on the Cross*
Rico Lebrun, *The Crucifixion*
Rubens, *The Descent from the Cross*
Rembrandt, *The Descent from the Cross*
Emil Nolde, *The Entombment*
Matthias Grunewald, *The Risen Christ*
Piero della Francesca, *The Resurrection*

Banners add to the festive note of the Easter service. Resurrection themes are the most appropriate, but any Christian message is fitting. The banners may simply read "He Lives," "He's Alive," "Christ the Lord Is Risen Today," "The Tomb Is Empty," "Joy," or "Rejoice! Christ Lives." The proper symbolism for these banners are the Lamb, the simple Latin or Greek cross, the cross of triumph, or the Sun.

Obviously the Scripture lesson for today will be the resurrection narratives. Selected lessons from the entry into Jerusalem to the resurrection appearances may be read. Or a special reading combining some of this material with other material may be prepared. The responsive reading allows members of the congregation to read the central Gospel responses to the resurrection; it allows them to be other than mere spectators to this central event.

Some of the selected lessons from Matthew might be taken from the following events and utilized on Palm Sunday or Easter.

The entry into Jerusalem, Matthew 21:1-11
The priests challenge Jesus, Matthew 21:23-27
The Pharisees question him about the great commandment, Matthew 22:35-40
The rulers conspire to kill Jesus, Matthew 26:3-5
Jesus prepares for the Passover, Matthew 26:17-30
Jesus agonizes in Gethsemane, Matthew 26:36-46
Judas betrays Jesus, Matthew 26:47-50
Jesus is taken to Pilate, Matthew 27:1-2, 11-14
Jesus is sent to be crucified, Matthew 27:26-37
Jesus dies and is buried, Matthew 27:50, 57-60
The resurrection, Matthew 28:1-6

Pentecost

The celebration of Pentecost is another intense moment in Christian worship. The main themes of Pentecost are power, evangelism, mission, and spiritual development (fruit of the Spirit). There is even a fellowship and social emphasis: "And all that believed were together, and had all things common" (Acts 2:44). These themes can form the basis for the music and the sermon. With such themes you can discover several fitting elements for the service: music, preaching, personal testimony, and readings of Acts 2 (in its entirety, perhaps responsively).

Banners from Pentecost can show the traditional "flame" (tongues of fire), the descending dove, or can carry the themes of the fruit of the Spirit (love, joy, etc.). If you should choose to emphasize that the Holy Spirit has come to empower the church to be on mission, the banner could bear the Jerusalem cross, an old symbol for the missionary challenge.

The Sunday Service

You may want to consider not having a printed "order" of worship for this service. This will suggest the surprise element which Pentecost presents. If you do print the elements of the service, keep it simple. Here is an example:

> Call to worship and prayer (see calls to worship,
>   chapter 1)
> Congregational singing
> The first Pentecost (Acts 2)
> Personal testimonies
> Sermon
> Invitation and challenge

Congregational singing for Pentecost can add to the spontaneous and participatory aspects so necessary to the success of this worship service. Probably, more than the usual number of hymns in your regular service ought to be sung. Fortunately, the number of appropriate hymns for Pentecost abounds. A hymnal in my house includes fifteen missionary hymns and eight about the Spirit. There also are many songs about love, joy, and peace. These hymns are of both the formal and informal kinds.

Personal testimonies are personal and therefore original. They may be spontaneous or planned. If your congregation is accustomed to unplanned elements in worship, the spontaneous testimonies will be the most appropriate. If you think the request for on-the-spot testimonies would result only in a long silence, then the persons whom you want to testify can be enlisted ahead of time.

The idea of the challenge at the end of service is to call the worshipers to go into the world as persons led by the Holy Spirit. The shape of the challenge will be determined by the sermon subject. For example, if the sermon subject is on the fruit of the Spirit, the challenge will go something like this (in your own style, of course).

This has been a special day in a long and inspiring series. At Christmas we celebrated the birth of our Lord Jesus Christ. We sang our favorite carols and heard again the familiar stories of the birth of Jesus. Then, in preparation for Easter, we submitted ourselves to spiritual disciplines and engaged in an intense study of the central doctrines of our faith. On Palm Sunday we waved the fronds and worshiped in joy. Toward the end of Holy Week we celebrated the Lord's Supper, reenacting Jesus' last supper with his disciples, and we experienced in our minds some of the fickleness which brought persons to turn against Jesus. The darkness of Good Friday came upon us, as it did those who loved Jesus and were with him to the end. We met in this sanctuary and snuffed candles representing the attempt to extinguish the teachings of Jesus at his death. On Saturday we waited for God to enter the drama. And then came Easter morning, and the stone was rolled from the door of the tomb. The Christ arose, and we brought out our highest praise. For fifty days now we have lived in the Easter light and have shared it with others. Then today we celebrated again, and this time it was the gift of the Spirit in power. We read how this Spirit overwhelmed the earliest Christians. Therefore, let us go into the world and exemplify the fruit of the Spirit. Let us be loving, joyful, peaceful, long-suffering, gentle, and live in goodness and faith.

The Lay Witness

Another idea for a Pentecost emphasis is the lay witness. You can't read Acts 2 without being impressed by the widespread excitement the earliest Christians had for the gospel—its effect in their own lives and its relevance to the world. That really is what the lay witness is—an activity in which lay persons tell how God is at work in their lives or how they are growing (or not growing) as Christians. It may include, but ought not to focus on, the conversion experience. The idea is to get your members to think theologically, that is, to put into a theological perspective what is happening to them, not at "church," but in all of their relationships and activities. This can be a revitalizing experience for any church.

The witnesses may be your own church members or Christians from other churches. In either case the lay persons share their faith, then dialogue with the group about their witness. By restricting the presentations to about ten minutes and having two persons to do the witnessing, you will help the lay persons avoid attempting to preach a well-organized sermon with text and poem. In fact, that is just what you want to avoid. Many lay persons would be frightened at preaching; others would hide behind sermonizing, thus refusing to get at their own religious experience.

The lay witness is simply a sharing of one's faith with persons inside and outside the church. It may begin or end on Pentecost Sunday. There is tradition for the Pentecost season being either the time from Easter to Pentecost Sunday or from Pentecost and after (also called Trinity season).

Some churches may want this time to be a revival season. What was said of the lay witness above applies equally to the revival. Both are strengthening to the fellowship and are essentially evangelistic. Can you find a more life-giving stimulus for Pentecost than seeing the Lord add to the church those who are being saved?

Chapter 7

Worship Service Outlines

Here are some outlines of worship services. Within these the variations are limitless. For example, the entire offertory time may follow different sequences.

Hymn/Prayer (or Sentence)/Collection
Hymn/Collection/Prayer (or Sentence)
Prayer (or Sentence)/Collection/Hymn

We have seen already that calls to worship may be spoken or sung and that spoken calls may be given by a single person or responsively. The lessons and readings in the services may also be read by one person or be done antiphonally. The Gloria Patri or the Doxology may be sung at appropriate times in the service, such as after a prayer, after the collection, at the end of the service, or after a psalm.

Simple Outline

Prayers and Congregational Singing
Offering and Doxology
Sermon and Invitation

Elements Without Categories

Call to Worship
Hymn
Invocation
Hymn
Scripture Reading
Pastoral Prayer

Offertory Hymn
Collection
Choral Music
Sermon
Invitation

Elements Embellished

The Prelude (Organ or Piano)
The Call to Worship (Spoken or Choral)
The First Hymn
The Invocation
The Second Hymn
The Lesson (New Testament or Old Testament)
The Pastoral Prayer
The Offertory Hymn
Offering
The Choral Music
The Sermon
The Invitation Hymn
The Benediction

A More Formal Alternative

The Prelude
The Introit
The Kyrie Eleison
The Gloria Patri
The Collect
The Epistle
The Gradual
The Collection Hymn
The Collection Sentence
The Collection
The Choral Celebration
The Sermon
The Hymn of Response
The Benediction

The *introit* has evolved into a combination of the processional and call to worship, although a call to worship may follow it in the order of worship. The *introit* is most appropriately a musical piece, sung antiphonally. It may be a psalm or a hymn emphasizing the season being celebrated in the worship service.

The *Kyrie Eleison,* "Lord, have mercy," may be used most effectively at the beginning of seasons of repentance, such as Lent, or in a Holy Week service. It can take many forms, such as the following.

Liturgist: All have sinned.
Congregation: Lord, have mercy upon us.
Liturgist: The wages of sin is death.
Congregation: Lord, have mercy upon us.

The *collect* is a pastoral prayer and includes elements of what is commonly called "directed" prayer.

The *gradual* is a musical response to the epistle. In the absence of a regular chant, a congregational hymn on the epistle will keep faith with the function of the *gradual.*

With Functional Categories

The Call to Worship
    The Prelude (Organ or Piano)
    The Spoken Call (or Musical)
    The Hymn of Praise
    The Invocation
The Lessons
    The Old Testament Lesson
    The New Testament Lesson
    The Hymn on the Lessons
The Offerings
    The Pastoral Prayer
    The Offertory Hymn
    The Giving of Money (The Collection)
The Word of God
    The Choral Music
    The Sermon
    The Hymn of Response
The Benediction
    Pastoral Notes
    The Benediction
    The Postlude (Organ or Piano)

With Uniform Functional Categories

Call to Worship
    Prelude
    Choral Call to Worship
Worship in Praise

Hymn
Invocation
Psalm
(Choral Praise)
Worship in Giving
Pastoral Prayer
Offertory Hymn
Offering
Worship in Proclamation
Scripture Reading (Single or Responsive)
(Choral Music)
Sermon
Invitation
Benediction
Prayer
Postlude

With Functional-Interpretive Categories

We Come to Worship
Prelude
Hymn (e.g., "O Worship the King")
Invocation
We Praise God
Psalm
Hymn
We Bring Our Gifts
(The children sing.)
(A youth plays an instrument or dances.)
(An adult gives a witness.)
Offertory Hymn and Offering
We Hear God's Word
Scripture
Sermon
Invitation
Benediction
Postlude

With Interpretive Categories

Our Movement Toward God
Prelude
Invitation to Worship
Hymn

Invocation
Hymn
Pastoral Prayer
Choral Music
God's Movement Toward Us
  Scripture Reading
  Message
Our Response
  Invitation Hymn
  Offering
  Benediction
  Postlude

● ● ●

Coming from the World
  Prelude
  Call to Worship
  Hymn
  Invocation
  Offertory Hymn
  Offering
Praising God
  Psalm
  Hymn
  Choral, Instrumental, Rhythmic, Praise, or Spontaneous
    Testimonies
Hearing God's Word
  Scripture
  Sermon
Returning to the World
  Hymn of Resolution (or Commitment, Loyalty, Service, etc.)
  Benediction
  Postlude

● ● ●

Call to Worship
  Prelude
  Call
  Hymn
  Invocation
God Speaks to Us
  Old Testament Lesson
  New Testament Lesson
  Sermon

We Speak Back
  Invitation Hymn
  Testimonies
  Hymn of Praise (Choir)
  Prayer of Praise (Some Dramatic Praise Expression)
  Offertory Hymn
  Offering
  Benediction

With Categories on a Theme

Call to the Word
  Prelude
  Call to Worship
  Hymn
  Invocation
Hearing the Word
  Old Testament Lesson
  New Testament Lesson
  Contemporary Lesson
  Anthem
The Word Interpreted
  Sermon
The Call of the Word
  Invitation to Respond
  Invitation Hymn
  Invitation to Give
  Offertory Hymn
  Benediction
  Postlude

The Traditional Worship Categories

Prelude
Penance (Confession)
  Scripture (or Excerpt from Religious Literature, e.g.,
    Augustine's *Confessions)*
  Hymn (Solemn)
  Prayer (Directed Prayer)
Praise (Thanksgiving)
  Psalm (or Poem)
  Hymn (Praise)
  Prayer
Petition

Congregational Needs
Pastoral Prayer
Choral Music (e.g., on Petition)
Offertory Hymn
Offering
Proclamation (Witness)
Scripture
Sermon
Invitation Hymn
Benediction

On the Functions of a Church

Worship
Prelude
Call to Worship
Hymn
Invocation
Teach
Old Testament Lesson
New Testament Lesson
Hymn
Proclaim
Choral Anthem
Sermon
Invitation Hymn
Serve
Offertory Hymn
Offering
Call to Go into the World
Benediction
Postlude

A Service Outlined by Hymn Verses

When I Survey the Wondrous Cross
Hymn (on the Cross)
Invocation
New Testament Reading (the Crucifixion)
My Richest Gain I Count but Loss
Hymn (on Service, Ministry)
Offertory Prayer
Offering
Sorrow and Love Flow Mingled Down

 Sermon (The Suffering Servant/The Suffering of
  Jesus)
Demands My Soul, My Life, My All
 Invitation Hymn
 Benediction

A Service Outlined by Bible Verses

Make a Joyful Noise to the Lord
 Call to Worship
 Hymn of Praise
 Invocation
Serve the Lord with Gladness
 Reading (Responsive) on Service
 Hymn of Service
 Offertory Sentence (or Prayer)
 Offering
Know That the Lord Is God
 Old Testament Reading
 Choral Music
It Is He That Hath Made Us
 Sermon (on Man/World Crises/People of God)
 Invitation
Be Thankful to Him
 Benediction
 Doxology

Notes

Chapter 1
[1] From the hymn "How Firm a Foundation."

Chapter 3
[1] From the hymn "Mighty God, While Angels Bless Thee."
[2] Samuel H. Miller, *The Dilemma of Modern Belief* (New York: Harper & Row, Publishers, 1963), p. 78.
[3] Joseph Machlis, *The Enjoyment of Music* (New York: W. W. Norton & Co., Inc., 1970), p. 420.

Chapter 4
[1] From the hymn "Trust, Try, and Prove Me," copyrighted © 1923 by Charles H. Gabriel.
[2] From the hymn "We Give Thee But Thine Own."

Chapter 5
[1] The sources of the quotes in this reading are as follows: Sir Walter Scott, "The Lay of the Last Minstrel"; "The Star-Spangled Banner"; "America"; "America the Beautiful"; Declaration of Independence; Rudyard Kipling, "Recessional"; "America the Beautiful"; Rudyard Kipling, "Children's Song"; the Constitution; Patrick Henry; Martin Luther King, Jr., *The Trumpet of Conscience* (New York: Harper & Row, Publishers, 1967), p. 77; from the hymn "God of Grace and God of Glory."
[2] The sources of the quotes in this reading are as follows: 1 Peter 2:9 (RSV); Psalm 100:3; Matthew 13:16; paraphrase of Matthew 25:40; Genesis 1:26; Luke 9:58 (RSV); paraphrase of Matthew 28:19, 20; from the hymn "Lead On, O King Eternal."

Bibliography

Cross, F. L., and Livingstone, E. A., *The Oxford Dictionary of the Christian Church,* 2nd ed. New York: Oxford University Press, 1974.

Davies, J. G., ed., *A Dictionary of Liturgy and Worship.* New York: Macmillan, Inc., 1972.

Dunkle, William F., *Values in the Church Year.* Nashville: Abingdon Press, 1959.

Emswiler, Sharon, and Emswiler, Thomas Neufer, *Women and Worship.* New York: Harper & Row, Publishers, 1974.

Encyclopaedia Britannica, Macropaedia, Volume 4. Chicago: Encyclopaedia Britannica Educational Corp., affiliate of Encyclopedia Britannica, Inc., 1977.

Encyclopaedia Britannica, Micropaedia, Volume 6. Chicago: Encyclopaedia Britannica Educational Corp., affiliate of Encyclopedia Britannica, Inc., 1977.

"Inclusive Language Resources." Order from Church Leadership Resources, Box 179, St. Louis, MO 63166.

Jungmann, Josef A., *The Early Liturgy.* Translated by Frances A. Brunner. London: Darton, Longman & Todd, 1959.

New Catholic Encyclopedia, Volume 8. New York: McGraw-Hill, 1967.

Podhradsky, Gerhard, *New Dictionary of the Liturgy.* London: Geoffrey Chapman, 1967.

Robinson, John A. T., *Christ Comes In.* London: A. R. Mowbray & Co., 1960.

Schaff, Philip, and Herzog, Johann, *The New Schaff-Herzog Encyclopedia,* Volumes 5 and 6. Grand Rapids: Baker Book House, 1960.

Spencer, Donald A., comp., *Hymn and Scripture Selection Guide.* Valley Forge: Judson Press, 1977.

Spielmann, Richard M., *History of Christian Worship.* New York: The Seabury Press, Inc., 1966.

Swidler, Arlene, ed., *Sistercelebrations: Nine Worship Experiences.* Philadelphia: Fortress Press, 1974.

Index